Australia Phoenix: 2053

How a nation survived climate change

Australia Phoenix: 2053

How a nation survived climate change

DAVID MORGAN

Copyright © 2013 David Morgan

All rights reserved.

ISBN-10: 1484 13740X
ISBN-13: 978-1484 137406

Cover illustration: Sidney Nolan, *Pretty Polly Mine*
by permission of Art Gallery of NSW

DEDICATION

For Elisabeth and Hanneke, who I pray will live to see how the story truly ends.

CONTENTS

PREFACE	1
CHRONOLOGY	7
ONE Lessons from the Dreamtime	8
TWO Lost in the middle of the journey	23
THREE The darkest hour	41
FOUR A lifeboat	61
FIVE This fortress	79
SIX A brave new world	96
POSTSCRIPT Australia Felix	112

ACKNOWLEDGMENTS

My thanks to Bronwyn Townsend, Des Dornan and Rick Jefferys for their thoughtful advice and encouragement all through this project. Thanks also to Jonathan Williams, Peter Long, Kathy Plume, Evan Townsend, Elisabeth and Hanneke Morgan for commenting on drafts, to Julie Roberts for her last words, and to all those who knowingly or unknowingly have contributed ideas to this synthesis. Ruth Flur has been a wise and critical editorial consultant, and any errors which remain are of my own doing. Finally my thanks to Elaine for keeping her feet on the ground and her mind in the present while I had my head in the clouds.

PREFACE

"Australian history is always picturesque; indeed, it is so curious and strange, that it is itself the chiefest novelty the country has to offer.... it does not read like history, but like the most beautiful lies".[1]

Each year since 1959, a series of six radio lectures has been delivered by prominent Australians. I presented the lectures of 2053, published now in the form of a book, which outline the history of Australia's place in recent world events, told from my own point of view as an eyewitness and respondent to climate change. Why did I choose to revisit these events, which have been described and assessed many times over?

Forty years ago, I wrote a small book, also called *Australia Phoenix:2053,*[2] which warned of the urgent need to prepare for climate change. I had learned, in my career as a civil engineer and builder, to look at problems in a multidisciplinary way, and to make connections between diverse data that specialists did not see. Some schooling in geology helped me to think in terms of the eras of natural history, rather than the span of a human life or a civilisation. Thus I was able to draw a coherent yet frightening picture of a plausible scenario of the future. It was read, initially by Australians, and then by a wider readership, people like me who were becoming increasingly concerned about the prognosis for life as we knew it. The challenges the book put forward became the subject of an ever-widening discussion. The result, thankfully, was urgent national action in Australia to prepare for what lay ahead.

---

[1] Mark Twain, *Following the Equator*
[2] David Morgan, *Australia Phoenix: 2053*

The question I still ask myself almost every day is, how as a species, watching this crisis unfold in the first decades of this century, did we do so little to prepare for it? How did it happen that eight billion intelligent, thinking people very nearly allowed their species and their world to be obliterated? My objective in retelling this appalling tragedy is to reflect on the seeming inability of humans to prepare for the future; it is also to show what I tried to show many years ago – that history repeats itself, that everything which happened to us has been endured in past times, and that we are not immune to the forces of history.

Of course it is in our nature to be short-sighted. Mankind is hard-wired to make tough, painful decisions only under duress. Our short-term focus and reactions derive from our evolution as hunter-gatherers. The concept of democratic government does not encourage the painful decisions that are necessary to assure welfare in the longer term. We were arrogant and overconfident to assume that our era would never end, and to think that we could not possibly be fated to live at the time of such a rare event as a climate turning point. In short, our complacency became deadly.

The worldwide crisis that emerged in the second decade of the century was really three crises in one – financial collapse, climate change and population decline. Our economies were based on the concept of 'something for nothing', investment horizons were too short, and we discounted future costs and future benefits. The global financial crash in 2016 – what I will term the 'Crash' – woke up Australia; ironically, it was the alarm that saved mankind, although at the time it seemed as though it had condemned us to an age of darkness. Global cooperation was shattered, international credit and trade collapsed, and nation states were thrown back on their own resources.

The signals of impending doom were obvious, if only we had chosen to see them; the concentration of carbon dioxide, carbon and methane in the atmosphere was increasing. We had exceeded key parameters within which we had lived during the previous 10,000 years. We thought we could bargain with nature, set carbon dioxide limits, and lived in the hope that stability would prevail. Few recognised that the Earth, or Gaia, was a series of interacting systems, making up a single huge ecosystem that behaved in a non-linear manner. Most of us had no understanding of the logic of the system. How could we? Too few of us had any understanding of systems theory, and took it all for granted, just as we did the operation of the many manufacturing processes, machines, telecommunications and computing devices upon which we had come to rely.

The last half of the twentieth century had been one of Elysian calm. Most people lived comfortable, healthy lives, prosperity grew, and the population of the world multiplied from two and a half to seven billion, thanks to improvements in medicine, pharmacology, public sanitation and agriculture. Industry and technical invention grew. Trade and the global economy expanded. But a series of earlier cataclysmic events – two world wars, the depression of the 1930s, the depredations of the Spanish flu epidemic in which fifty million people lost their lives, and the tragic upheavals of Chinese society during Mao's Cultural Revolution – should have shown us that we were not God's chosen race, and that God would not intervene to save us from disaster. Uncountable species have become extinct in the course of geological history; why did we not understand that ours could too?

There are few heroes, few individuals, named in this history. That is because I believe that history is not driven by great individuals, but by the combined power of many nameless persons, responding and adapting to events. The impetus for change comes from changes in our environment, climate and the geological behaviour of the Earth. The great personalities of history are, in my view, merely reflecting the mood of their society at the time.

> You must admit that the genesis of the great man depends on the long series of complex influences which has produced the race in which he appears, and the social state into which that race has slowly grown ... Before he can remake his society, his society must make him.[3]

It is ironic and regrettable that the phrases 'great individual' and 'great man' are used interchangeably. Half of humanity is women, yet their fifty-percent contribution to history is largely ignored. As much history is written in the bedrooms and nurseries as on the battlefields or in political assemblies. So even the 'great man' theory of history implicitly neglects the anonymous contribution of many billions of women.

To my mind, what drives history is what Adam Smith called the 'invisible hand'; it is the sum total of the response of many individuals, making their own choices, both intentionally and involuntarily. How do these trends and patterns start? Who initiates them? How do they proliferate? Successful societies seem to have a genius for experimenting with alternatives, and a flexibility that allows them to adapt behaviour to what delivers success.

When faced with catastrophic change, those nations, like France, which had retained all the building blocks of an economy – manufacturing, food production, energy supply, health care – were able to hunker down into self-sufficiency. Others, such as the UK, which by 2016 relied on imports for 75% of its energy and

---

[3] Herbert Spencer, *The Study of Sociology*, 1873

50% of its food, fell into chaos. Australia, self-sufficient in the basic human needs of water, food and energy, was eventually able to overcome the loss of essential technologies and manufacturing capability, although the early years were tough. Less adaptable societies, beset by conflict or disorganisation, did not survive.

> Stress drives evolution. Extinction occurs when an organism fails to adapt to change in the environment.[4]

The concepts of evolution are as applicable to societies as they are to living organisms. The successful are rewarded by survival, the unsuccessful fail. Under stress, adaptable beings evolve to fit the new environment, while those unable to test new responses and to change, fail. Nature is unsentimental, and yet it rewards innovation and collaboration.

Through it all, I have always hoped that, just as the sunflower turns its head every day to follow the sun, humanity has an innate compass which turns its soul towards a universal beacon of truth and spiritual growth. How else can we have travelled this far in such a capricious and risky universe?

What follows is a story of loss, survival and rebirth.

---

[4] P. A. Parsons, *Nature 351*, pp 356-357

CHRONOLOGY

Years ago

3,400 million   Formation of the Earth

34-56 million   Eocene epoch

2.6 million   Beginning of last Ice Age, or Quarternary Period

73,000   Mount Toba erupts, triggering onset of glaciation

60,000   Human settlement of Australia

15,000, 11,000 and 8,000 years   Melting events gradually end glaciation

Date

1788   European settlement of Australia

1901   Federation of the Australian States

1929   Great Depression begins

2008   Global financial crisis

2014   Collapse of the Euro currency

2016   Global economic crash triggers global depression

2019   Burning of Amazonia, Abu Dhabi gas cloud

2020   Collapse of Tarbela dam

                                 Australian National Constitutional Convention

2022   Atlantic tsunami hits east coast of Americas

2031   Eruption of volcanos in Iceland and South America,

                                 Onset of Anthropocene Glaciation

2040   Destruction of Darwin by suitcase atomic weapon

2053   Australia Phoenix radio lectures broadcast

ONE

Lessons from the Dreamtime

According to Aboriginal belief, all life as it is today – Human, Animal, Bird and Fish – is part of one vast unchanging network of relationships which can be traced to the great spirit ancestors of the Dreamtime.[5]

Caught unawares

The history of glaciation – the cycles of warming and freezing that the Earth has undergone – has been known to us for many years. We can chart changes in glacial activity with reasonable accuracy from the study of cores drilled out of the ancient icecaps of Antarctica and Greenland. How is it then, in our current era, that most of the world has been caught unawares by the nature and severity of climate change? Why did we assume that the likelihood of climate change was negligible, when glaciations, interglacials, mass migrations and species extinctions were so common and had occurred so relatively recently? Was it arrogance, or complacency, to assume that geological change would pass us by, and that the interglacial would last for eternity? How was it, in recent times, that some societies of genius, Australia among them, were able to survive the chaos and destruction of climate change? And how close did we come to annihilation? These are some of the questions which I will consider in these broadcasts.

---

[5] www.aboriginalart.com

Ice

It is the year 2053. We live in an ice age. The Quarternary-Pleistocene Glaciation began 2.6 million years ago, around about the time that evolution was creating the precursors of our species; since that time, the Earth has experienced eighteen cycles of glaciation, of roughly equal duration. Glacials, or colder periods, have alternated with warmer periods, known as interglacials. During each glacial, the oceans shrank as huge quantities of water were turned to snow and stored in polar ice caps. Then, with each interglacial, the ice retreated, sea levels rose, and the continents flexed as they adjusted their levels to the changed weight of the ice overburden. Earthquakes and volcanoes were unleashed, cooling the Earth with shrouds of dust. All the time life went on adapting under the stress of climate change.

This history begins only 110,000 years ago, at the beginning of the last cycle – the Wurm Glaciation. At the height of the Wurm, much of northern Europe, Russia and North America were frozen under permanent ice caps. In the southern hemisphere, Antarctica was larger, and permanent glaciers covered the Andes, the Australian Alps, and the highlands of Irian Jaya. The end of the Wurm Glaciation was marked by three major, sudden ice melting and sea level increases occurring 15,000, 11,000 and 8,000 years ago. We can read descriptions of the most recent melting in Plato's description of Solon's warning to the Greeks of great floods, in the legends of Noah and Gilgamesh and in the Rig Veda.

> Like the rest of mankind you have suffered from convulsions of nature, which are chiefly brought about by the two great agencies of fire and water.[6]

Mankind survived the long upheavals of the Wurm, but our competitor, the Neanderthal species, became extinct. This era, but

---

[6] Plato, *Timaeus*

a moment in geological terms, shaped who we are and where we live on the planet, giving rise to what we call 'civilisation'.

Fire

Just as much as glaciation, volcanic activity has also had a profound effect on geology and the course of human history. There is clear evidence that the Little Ice Age, from the thirteenth to the sixteenth century A.D., was caused by a short period of intense, explosive vulcanism. Aerosol particles ejected by volcanos chilled the northern hemisphere, increasing the area of polar sea ice, reflecting more sunlight and slowing the flow of warmer water to the north. Average summer temperatures in the northern hemisphere did not return until the twentieth century. In fact, it is clear from polar ice-core analysis that glaciation and volcanic activity have consistently acted in tandem. The largest single eruption in the last 110,000 years, of one of the world's larger volcanoes, Mt Toba in Indonesia, occurred only 73,000 ($\pm$4,000) years ago. To get some conception of its magnitude, imagine an explosion 10,000 times greater than Mt St Helens, which erupted in the western USA in 1990.

The eruption produced a gigantic plume of ash and sulphur oxides which dispersed to the west and north-west, cloaking the Earth in shadow, causing a six-year continuous winter, and triggering the instant onset of a savage 1,000 year glacial peak. The whole of India was covered in a layer of ash 150 mm thick. Almost the whole of south-east Asia was deforested. Mankind, wherever he was, died in huge numbers from cold and famine, except for a small group of some 10,000 people who survived in equatorial Africa.

Man on the move

With the eruption, there began a series of changes which led to the first settlement of Australia by human beings. The story goes like this. Before Toba, Neanderthal man occupied southern Europe, in equilibrium with humans who inhabited the tropics, the Indian subcontinent and Africa. The Neanderthals were better adapted to the cold, and lived in marginal regions where humans could not thrive. The glacial peak caused by Toba almost eliminated the habitat in which man could survive; human life everywhere was extinguished by the cold, except for a very few, perhaps only 1,000 to 10,000 breeding pairs, who survived, and were isolated and confined in a small habitable region of equatorial Africa. The survival of our species was a very close-run affair, and the risk of extinction far greater than it ever was during the major cataclysms and global wars of more recent eras. It is chilling to think about it now, although it's easy to understand what a remote possibility it would have seemed in 2012, when the Earth's population reached 7 billion.

In Africa, subject to the stress of survival in a harsh environment, forced to compete for scarce resources, the best adapted to the struggle for survival were selected by the evolutionary process. Intelligence, collaboration and teamwork were rewarded.[7] As the climate relented, plant and animal life returned to the defoliated lands. This was still a glacial period, so sea levels were much lower than they are now, and wide sweeping coastal shelves were exposed around the coasts of Africa and Asia. The boundary constraints of desert gradually receded, the population began to increase again and people commenced an outward migration around the coastal margins of Africa, the subcontinent, south-east asia and eventually across the land bridge to Australia.[8]

---

[7] 'When the Sea Saved Humanity', Curtis W. Marean, *Scientific American* August 2010
[8] 'Rise of the Modern Mind', *New Scientist*, 6 November 2010

The first Australians

We will never know for sure exactly when these people arrived in Australia, although it is certain that they were the first. The approximate timing comes to us indirectly from the extinction of the Australian megafauna, or large animals; before the arrival of man, giant marsupials existed in similar ecological niches to the giant mammals of Europe and Asia. We can date the period of only a few thousand years when these larger animals were hunted to extinction. And then an astonishing thing happened: the environmental depredation ended. The early people invented a way of living in harmony with the remaining natural environment, and were able to sustain this for some 60,000 years.

Who were they? What do we know of how they existed during these 60,000 years?[9] What can we learn from them? From what we do know, we must draw as many lessons as we can from their example for our own future.

So many questions

We do not know how the aboriginal tribes responded to the climate changes that must have taken place as the Wurm glaciation waxed and waned. Nor do we know how they were affected by the volcanoes which created the extensive lava fields of southern and south-western Victoria, or a coastline which broadened and narrowed as sea levels rose and fell. The people who were isolated on Tasmania, when the sea level finally rose ten thousand years ago, were found with some divergence from the mainland race; fish had dropped out of their menu, and the use of stone tools had vanished.

They left no written history, no chronicles, and their knowledge, which was transmitted by mouth, is largely lost. We have done a

---

[9] History of Indigenous Australians, *Wikipedia*

pitifully small amount of archaeology, owing, I believe, to a lack of respect, even though there is still no shortage of remains. The coastal margins and the banks of inland water courses are peppered with the ash beds of their cooking fires containing discarded shells and bones. It seems we found the 'early civilisations' of the great rivers – the Harrapan of the Indus, Mesopotamia and ancient Egypt – so much more interesting because they were culturally closer to us.

By and large, we think they lived in *stasis*, with limited change and little innovation after the initial adaptation to the new continent. The use of stone tools continued with minor changes in style. Art styles, or at least rock art styles, changed over time. The use of the boomerang continued; boomerangs of similar design have been found in the tombs of ancient Egyptian kings so this technology must date back at least to the time when the two streams of migration out of Africa diverged.

Nomads

Most of what we know comes from a few accounts written by perceptive early settlers and the accounts of missionaries who worked in the interior with the more isolated tribes.

> At sunset, a party of a score of the black aborigines passed by, each carrying, in their accustomed manner, a bundle of spears and other weapons. By giving a leading young man a shilling, they were easily detained, and threw their spears for my amusement. They were all partly clothed, and several could speak a little English: their countenances were good-humoured and pleasant, and they appeared far from being such utterly degraded beings as they have usually been represented. In their own arts they are admirable. A cap being fixed at thirty yards distance, they transfixed it with a spear, delivered by the throwing-stick with the rapidity of an arrow from the bow of a practised archer. In tracking animals or men they show most wonderful sagacity; and I heard of several of their

remarks which manifested considerable acuteness. They will not, however, cultivate the ground, or build houses and remain stationary, or even take the trouble of tending a flock of sheep when given to them.[10]

Social organisation was tribal. Although small, the population encompassed more than 750 languages or dialects, and as many social groupings, each jealously husbanding their own territory for sustenance. People lived and moved with the seasons, following the availability of food – wild plants and game. Despite existing in small social units, there was commerce and intercourse between the tribes. Scarce materials and tools were traded across the country. Languages were mutually intelligible and the tribes intermarried. The continent was linked by a network of *songlines*, ancient routes mapped by means of symbolism and song.

Estimates of the population range between a half and one million; compare this with 20 million now and one can see that we have overstretched the natural carrying capacity of the land. The number of people was consciously controlled to avoid damage to food resources. But European settlement, which began in 1788, was deadly; by 1900 the indigenous population had declined by ninety percent. In 1870, only one aborigine remained in Tasmania. Today only a few remnants remain, largely inland and in the Northern Territory, many living in tragic circumstances. I can remember as a child seeing poverty-stricken black people camping on the river flats outside our town in ramshackle shelters called 'humpies'. They were later rehoused to a purpose-built village, but sadly lacked the skills or behaviours necessary to live in modern circumstances and to co-exist with European society.

In the early years of settlement, there were appalling battles and atrocities; this was the dark underside of European colonisation

---

[10] Charles Darwin, *The Voyage of the Beagle*

everywhere in the world. By far the largest loss of life was due to diseases transmitted by the new colonists from which the natives had no immunity. As Charles Darwin observed in an interesting reflection presaging *The Origin of the Species* by several decades, written during his voyage home in the *Beagle*:

> The number of aborigines is rapidly decreasing ... This decrease, no doubt, must be partly owing to the introduction of spirits, to European diseases (even the milder ones of which, such as the measles, prove very destructive), and to the gradual extinction of the wild animals. It is said that numbers of their children invariably perish in very early infancy from the effects of their wandering life; and as the difficulty of procuring food increases, so must their wandering habits increase; and hence the population, without any apparent deaths from famine, is repressed in a manner extremely sudden compared to what happens in civilised countries, where the father, though in adding to his labour he may injure himself, does not destroy his offspring. Besides these several evident causes of destruction, there appears to be some more mysterious agency generally at work. Wherever the European has trod, death seems to pursue the aboriginal. ...The varieties of man seem to act on each other in the same way as different species of animals — the stronger always extirpating the weaker.[11]

Gardeners

Continental Australia was the garden of the Australian aborigine. Their diet was good. It is thought that the average nomad had a larger frame and skull than modern man; people were on average more intelligent, as survival required the mastery of greater skills than for life in a city, where specialisation allowed a more collaborative and less stressful existence. Food was captured by hunting, fishing and gathering.[12] Fire was used routinely to clear undergrowth and create pasture for wildlife to be hunted later.

---

[11] Charles Darwin, *Origin of the Species*
[12] Australian National Botanic Gardens, Canberra, www.anbg.gov.au

Important foods were replanted. Fish traps were built, and in some cases fish were farmed; traps constructed on the upper Darling River are the oldest man-made structures on Earth. Plants were harvested for fruit, seeds and roots; treatment and cooking processes to remove poisons were sometimes complex. Vegetation also provided a host of resources: medicines, materials for fire lighters, baskets, mats, nets, dishes, buckets, boats, glue, weapons, shelter, musical instruments, paints, cosmetics, fire starters, jewels, cosmetics, knives and tools. Animals were hunted for food and clothing.

The people were socially sophisticated; strict rules governed marriage and the relationship between men and women, in order to preserve genetic diversity and control population size. I have tried to understand their kinship rules and found them impossibly complex, but then they may have found our common law to be equally opaque. Music, dance, painting and the decoration of their natural environment were pursued avidly. The people chose their own leaders based on their survival skills. Each tribe had a medicine specialist, who used many herbal treatments and simple surgical techniques. Tribes also employed expert dream interpreters, indicating an advanced degree of psychic understanding.

Land and resources were owned in common by the clan, with clearly defined and aggressively defended boundaries. Rules for the exploitation of resources were shared and passed down through the generations. Men collaborated in hunting parties, and women shared the gathering of food. Each family group had a headman or elder, who was the leader of the unit. He decided when to move camp and he settled disputes. The headman's judgements were enforced by a range of sanctions, the most severe being to wound or to kill. Although inter-clan disputes occurred, inter-clan co-operation was prevalent, implying mutual respect of land rights. As far as we know, there was never any form of federation of clans or national government.

A long view

Throughout my life, whenever I was in England, I took delight in attending evensong in one of the great cathedrals. It gave me a sense of the stability and continuity of English society, to imagine this ceremony taking place in this building, continuously, for the last one thousand years. I experienced the same feeling sitting in the shadows within the great mosques of North Africa, imagining unbroken worship over almost fifteen hundred years, back almost to the time of the prophet Mohammed.

Now, can you imagine a world in which we are able to look back on not one thousand years or fifteen hundred but on sixty thousand years of continuity? On a world in which we have used the same dwellings, the same roads, the same tools, factories, farms, temples, literature, medicine, psychology, picture galleries, for sixty thousand years? The Australian aborigines did exactly that – they fashioned a society that endured for sixty millennia.

The 'tragedy of the commons'

Clearly, to have survived sustainably for 60,000 years, the aborigines must have found a solution to the 'tragedy of the commons'. 'The commons' are resources owned in common or shared by all members of a community. Traditionally the commons were lands owned by all and which all had a right to use freely. The so-called 'tragedy of the commons' occurs when many individuals, each exercising their rights, and acting in their own self-interest to use, for example, a common parcel of land, exhaust the commons through over-grazing or over exploitation. Modern cases include the over-fishing of the oceans, leading to exhaustion of fishing stock, the dumping of carbon dioxide into the atmosphere and over-population.

There is an interesting analogy between the unregulated exploitation of the commons and a cancer which grows uncontrollably in the body and destroys its host. Why does this happen in the case of a cancer and yet the healthy cells that make the organism itself limit their lifespan for the benefit of all? We have no idea, and yet it must be an agent of profound intelligence and altruism.

This predicament, how to manage the commons, was addressed many years ago by Elinor Ostrom,[13] the first woman to win the Nobel Prize in economics. Her life's work was the study of the economic management of commons. She investigated how the interaction of people with their ecosystems can be structured to maintain sustainable resource yields of common pool resources, such as forests, fisheries, oil and gas fields, grazing lands and irrigation resources. Her field studies considered pasture management in Africa and irrigation water management in Nepal. From this work, she identified the strategies which people have adopted to successfully manage resources and avoid ecosystem collapse; her eight design principles are as follows:

1. Define boundaries clearly to exclude unentitled persons
2. Have rules regarding access to and use of resources which fit local conditions
3. Use a shared decision-making process in which all users in the community participate
4. Appoint monitors who are accountable to the users for enforcing the rules
5. Apply a graduated scale of punishment for rule violation
6. Have a cheap, readily accessible dispute resolution process
7. The self-government rights of the community must be recognised by any higher authority
8. For larger resource pools, have an hierarchy of management organisations, with small communities at the lowest level.

---

[13] Elinor Ostrom, *Wikipedia*

In essence, resource management decisions should be made as close to the scene of events and participants as possible.

Events in Georgian England

Management of the commons was also a concern in Georgian England, where from around 1750, thirty-eight years before the European settlement of Australia and the beginning of the end of the Dreamtime, events took a course that would have profound consequences not only for the aborigines but for the whole world. Common lands had become overgrazed and exploited. At the behest of the ruling class, who dominated politics, Parliament passed the first of the Enclosure Acts. Traditional rights to graze, to harvest and to hunt, guaranteed since Anglo-Saxon times, were ended and the land expropriated by wealthy landowners.

Their expropriation of wealth brings to mind the recent self-centred behaviour of multi-national corporations and central governments. Compare the conduct of the Georgian aristocracy with the voracious grab of shareholders' funds in the form of bonuses, options and excessive salaries by the executives of large corporations in the final years before the economic crash in 2016.

A landless working class was created in England, and driven to the cities to labour in the new industries. Crime increased and the backlog of convicts held in prisons after the end of transportation to the American colonies grew. Settlement of a new penal colony in New South Wales became a convenient outlet.

> Manufactures underwent an expansion hitherto undreamed of, in order then to make way for the great industry, the steam engine, and the gigantic factories. Whole classes of the population disappeared, new classes took their place, with new conditions of life and new needs. [14]

---

[14] Karl Marx, *The English Revolution*

The end of 'localism'

The industrial revolution marked the beginning of another trend in human affairs, with the centralisation of industry and the distancing of ownership through the innovation of joint stock companies. Heretofore, throughout human history, industries had been decentralised. Every town had its own facilities and institutions, its market, bakery, forge, foundry, grain silo, mill, dairy, butter factory, brewery, tailor, boot-maker, cabinet-maker, woodsmen, blacksmith, public house and so on. Much later, towns had their own gasworks and electricity company. Except for the state and church, ownership of assets was local (the Roman Catholic church was the first multinational corporation). Farms were small, and supplied the markets in the towns. People worked from home, in cottage industries, making their own clothes, cutting their own wood. Towns and cities specialised in particular products: Ghent and Bruge wove wool, Antwerp made harpsichords, and they traded with each other. The cities of the Hanseatic League even established a trade and co-operation agreement. Specialised trade skills were maintained and jealously guarded by guilds.

The land carried far more people than it does now. There are still, in France and across Europe the remnants of countless deserted farms and towns, and their beautiful old masonry buildings, left behind in the migration to the big cities. Industrialisation changed evrything. Huge factories and works were built around the power output of fixed steam engines. The transport of heavy freight was also concentrated, first to canals then later to railways. Road transport took many years to catch up; this was before tarmacadam roads and motorised vehicles. The profitability of centralised industry led to further centralisation. Success drove centralisation of thought, and ultimately a global monoculture, which led to great distortions and aberrations, especially in government departments and major corporations.

Destruction of a civilisation

And so in the late eighteenth century forces far away in England took a course that would lead to, not only the destruction of the people of the Dreamtime, but, eventually, the world crisis from which we are now emerging in 2053. The Dreamtime ended a few short years after European settlement in 1788. Australia remained an insignificant, pastoral backwater until the discovery of gold and the rush of 1851. Thus, these people who had established a 60,000 year 'reich' in the great south land and mastered the management of the commons, lived their last years in paradise, before destruction by a more vigorous race lacking their social sophistication, but possessing a raw and ungovernable energy.

The dissipation of our resource bank

In the decades leading to the collapse of the global economy and financial system as we knew it, resources were increasingly not owned by local residents. The rights to exploit minerals were awarded to foreign companies who had no stake in local communities; residents were displaced from their lands, wealth was taken from the resources for use elsewhere, while waste products were disposed of locally. Pollution was dumped into the oceans and carbon dioxide into the atmosphere because they were commons owned by no-one. Countries located upstream of major rivers expropriated the flow of water for themselves, denying it to states downstream. Corporations chose to reside in supportive, benign communities, then did all in their power to avoid paying taxes in return for the security, stability and the licence to produce wealth which the community awarded.

Consequently, in the opening years of the twenty-first century, we found ourselves, without really reflecting upon the paradigm, captives of the huge centralisation of office work, manufacture, agriculture, electricity generation and water supply.

Instead of walking to work, we travelled long distances in motor cars on congested roads, burning hydrocarbon fuels. Only when we were forced to after the world financial crash of 2016 did it become obvious that environmental impact and economics actually favoured small industries owned at local level, just as Elinor Ostrom had advocated.

And so began the redirection of Australian society and industry from a global to a local orientation. We shall consider these profound changes in later chapters.

So where have we come to?

Let's return to the present time. It is 2053.

I began my history with the natural history of the current ice age and the story of the aboriginal peoples of Australia, who displayed wisdom exceeding more modern civilisations. My objective has been to shine a light on the folly of the western world, in the last decades of the twentieth century, in ignoring the severity of climate change events in our recent geological history. I wanted to show how we destroyed a distinctive cultural knowledge born of nature and our surroundings and instead adopted a universal cultural knowledge of technologies which attempted to dominate nature. By leading lives of unbridled selfishness, we had almost forgotten a way of life which did not impinge on the ecosystem of our planet.

It is not too late to learn from the few people still living a nomadic life. A more resilient Australian society will result if we can synthesise modern ways with wisdom gleaned from ancient societies. From the democratic governance of small communities, to medicine, microeconomics, land and woodland management, psychology and the law, our way of life may be enriched and strengthened by what those societies could teach us.

TWO

Lost in the middle of the journey

Nel mezzo del cammin di nostra vita

mi ritrovai per una selva oscura

che la ditta via era smarrita.[15]

The opening stanza of Dante's *Inferno* is an apt analogy for where we found ourselves in 2016, almost forty years ago on the journey of mankind, lost and exhausted from a long period of living beyond our means, economically as well as ecologically.

What were the causes of the great global Crash in 2016? How could an era that had brought us such prosperity end so abruptly? How did we allow an era which saw such a flowering of intellectual, social and economic development revert to chaos so easily? To understand the journey that led us to the 'Crash', I would like to return to the branch in the road which was chosen at the end of the Second World War and follow it to the economic catastrophe that occurred around seventy years later.

From World War to Cold War

The settlement of Europe was never fully resolved by the ending of World War II. Russia, leading the Soviet Union, established hegemony over the lands under its occupation when the fighting stopped. An armed standoff was engaged, between democratic west and communist east – the so-called 'Cold War'. It was a war

---

[15] Dante Alighieri, *La Divina Commedia* (In the middle of the journey of our lives, I found myself in a dark wood with the correct direction lost.)

of pure defence, with Europe the battleground, and both sides armed with enough nuclear weapons to assure total, mutual destruction. Thankfully, it remained 'cold'. I would like to think that this was not by accident, and that amongst all this folly there existed people wise enough to restrain the rest of us from the brink of the precipice. If so, it gives me hope for our future, now.

The USA emerged from the war in 1945 as the victor, with the other members of the successful alliance hugely in its debt. Just as the Soviet Union exercised control over the lands of Eastern Europe and Asia, so the USA imposed its economic dominance over the nations of the west. It was more subtle than Russia, and more successful. The USA imposed international institutions to support its agenda – the United Nations, the World Bank, the International Monetary Fund and the World Trade Organisation. These institutions were disguised in the mantle of democracy, but the underlying purpose was always to impose the capitalist system and assure American well-being. I cannot deny that there was a strong element of idealism in their zeal to promote liberal democracy. The restoration of the countries of their former enemies, Japan and Germany, was an act of altruism without precedent in history.

The Cold War, despite a near miss in the Cuban Missile Crisis of 1962, ended with the repudiation of the Russian communist model of Marxism and the economic exhaustion of the Soviet Union. Ronald Reagan deftly brought things to a close in 1991, heroically aided on the Russian side by Boris Yeltsin. So ended the 80-year experiment with communism that had begun with the Russian Revolution in 1917. At the time it was trumpeted as a triumph of the free world; it did seem like a victory, but the irony now is that Russia's attempt to create communism, although misguided and clumsy, can be seen as an attempt, one hundred years ahead of its time, to create a better way of being. It was unfortunate in the choice of men to lead it. It was unfortunate, too, in that Russia was not the place for social experiments of this sort, having struggled to make any form of national government work effectively.

In mainland China, Mao Tse Tung, having expelled the nationalists to Formosa (now Taiwan) in 1949, resolved on a crash programme – the so-called Great Leap Forward – to convert the state from an agrarian to an industrial economy. Agriculture was collectivised and the people were compelled to establish new industries. Mismanagement and chaos were enormous; 34 million people died between 1958 and 1962. Eventually, Mao was marginalised by more pragmatic men, but rebounded in 1966 with the Cultural Revolution. In the subsequent rampages of the Red Guard, perhaps another 20 million people lost their lives.

The disruption ended only with Mao's death in 1976. Intelligent men stepped forward, and opened China to the world. Thus began the growth of a new industrial superpower, motivated by capitalist principles and disciplined by the unyielding hegemony of the Communist Party. The Chinese peoples, subjugated and obedient, built world-class industries and a balance of international trade so substantial that eventually half the world came to be in their debt.

Pax Americana

The Cold War provided convenient justification for the military industrial complex in the USA to maintain the most formidable fighting forces the world had ever known; however, with capability came a proclivity to aggression. The USA involved itself in serial, unnecessary warfare, in Korea, Vietnam, Cuba, Nicaragua, Iraq, Afghanistan, Pakistan, Iran and beyond. These ventures were seldom successful. The American way of fighting was to employ blankets of firepower, supported by mammoth logistical operations, but more often than not it found itself defeated or stalemated by numerically weaker, more skilled, more determined, and more frugal opponents, who made every shot count. Such was the stranglehold of the American generals and military industrial complex on the US republic that through every failure, they continued, unashamed and unopposed, to destroy the lives of millions and suck vast amounts of money from the treasury.

At home, the American people, wealthy and in credit with the world, consumed resources excessively, particularly oil, which was burnt in huge quantities by automobiles on a continental road-transport system. For many years, the USA thrived, but at some time in the 1970s there emerged a complacency, an assumption that wealth and comfort were the birthright of the nation. The appetite for oil became an addiction, to be met at any cost. Government grew; spending on Medicare and Social Security (health and pensions) increased, and wealth was squandered on misguided foreign military adventures. Taxes were kept low, most especially for the rich. Many of the greatest names in American business conspired to avoid paying the taxes essential to support the state which provided them with a free-market haven for the accumulation of vast wealth. A strong dollar replaced gold as the reserve currency used by the whole world for trading. By 1986, however, dollar reserves were exhausted, and the USA began to borrow more than it was investing abroad. America had become addicted to comfort; an aging population paid even less tax than before and expected more social welfare. At first the deficit was modest, but as the economy slid into recession, businesses began to fail, particularly automotive manufacturers and banks. The government deficit grew, but borrowing remained easy, fed by willing trading partners, especially China.

American aggression abroad continued long beyond the time when the USA was able to afford it, and contributed substantially to the debt mountain. Afghanistan and Iran were the USA's last foreign military adventures, begun by George W. Bush; his greatest folly was to commit his country to unwinnable conflicts which had no bearing on American interests. Iran was empowered to become the sponsor of a destructive and anarchic campaign of global mischief and terrorism which preoccupied the great powers of the west for two decades. These lengthy US military incursions were financed, not by taxation or savings elsewhere in government expenditure, but by borrowing and reduced taxes. Resources that could have been invested in preparation for the coming climate change were, instead, squandered. China was the beneficiary, from both its position as lender, and from the increased global reach it acquired as the USA exhausted its people and finances.

It was scarcely credible to see a military confrontation emerging between China and the USA, in which China bankrolled its potential opponent – one of the poorest countries in the world lending to the richest! This to me was the greatest paradox of Chinese communism. It was ironic that the final precipitate defeat and collapse of global American military power resulted not from force of arms on the battlefield, but from the withdrawal of funding by holders of treasury bonds.

The brief flowering of globalism

Towards the end of the twentieth century, the global economic agenda was seized from Keynesian managers by the winner-takes-all, neo-liberal economists. Their central tenet was that the market was the best arbiter of supply and demand, and that businesses should be allowed to live or die depending on their ability to adapt and change.

Banks grew too large and lent far more money than they could ever hope to recover. It became easier for them to earn a profit by trading electronic money than through generating wealth by honest labour. The trading of financial derivatives was exploited to generate huge profits, but at enormous risk. High frequency trading generated money from nowhere. Foreign currency exchange, invented to facilitate international trade, became a game of risk and speculation. If a bank succumbed to these huge risks, it would threaten to bring the nation's economy down unless it was bailed out by government; because of globalisation, failure threatened not just individuals and corporations, but whole states. As each bank was saved, the rest, concluding that they could similarly get off free if things went wrong, continued to run themselves as casinos.

The neo-liberal free market principles which first legitimised casino banking were forgotten. The fatal flaw, or perhaps in more apt terms, the fatal dishonesty of the neo-liberal concept of free markets was to take the benefits, but evade adjustments and failures.

Corporations became global enterprises. The biggest had annual turnovers greater than the GDP of small nation states. Many were joint stock companies, but their ownership was wide and diluted. The shareholders of these hulking conglomerates were too distant, too numerous and too diffuse to understand or control the behaviour of their executives. These companies were dominated by egotistical and single-minded men, kleptocrats more interested in accumulating bonuses and honours than providing a social function for the community in which they had their homes. Can you believe that in 2010, of the one hundred highest-salaried chief executives in the USA, twenty-five took home more pay than their company paid in federal corporate income taxes? Self-appointed autocrats of industry, they rode the waves of plenty, ruled over vast, undemocratic empires and rewarded themselves compensation out of all proportion to their contribution to society.

Corporations had, by the first decade of the twenty-first century, become too big to control! Governments were blackmailed into bailing out failures with taxpayers' money, deferring the pain of adaptation and storing up much greater problems for the future. Corporations had privatised profits, but socialised their risks.

When it came to the crunch, the neo-liberals lost their nerve, and looked to the state to subsidise failure. In 2008, a few of the larger American banks were allowed to fail, but the rest were propped up with borrowed or printed money. In the UK, big banks were partly nationalised. Australia avoided the worst of the downturn because so much of its external income was derived from mining exports, and the products of the mines were in strong demand from the booming economies of south-east Asia.

Failure on an altogether larger scale was inevitable by 2016, because governments no longer had the resources to intervene.

The degeneration of democracy

By 2016, governments had become too distant to heed individuals. Electorates, as with shareholder rolls, were so large that the rights of individuals and small groups were trampled upon for the good of the corporation or government. The collusion between central governments and large companies had become so extensive that the legitimate concerns of communities were ignored:

- The USA committed itself and its allies to wars that had nothing to do with the interests of their citizens.
- The managers of the European Union attempted a grand scheme of unification which had more to do with centralised control than with ministering to the diverse interests of its peoples.
- Oil companies were allowed to poison the air and water, venturing even into the Arctic to explore that territory as soon as the polar ice cap had melted.

- Nuclear power authorities covered up safety deficiencies in order to preserve their existence.
- The rulers of China exploited their people to accumulate overseas wealth, while paying them little, polluting their environment and denying them many of the benefits of modernisation.

In Australia, governments of the day mistakenly associated their own existence with the national good. These times of plenty were unchallenging and the electorate's attention span was short. Governments were more concerned with the response of public opinion to tomorrows' headlines than they were with the judgement of history. Representatives of the people shied away from the difficult decisions they had been elected to make, infighting was endemic, and essential services such as flood protection, transport and energy supply were neglected. Some quite mediocre people came to power.

The ready availability of borrowed money enabled the rich countries of the west to live beyond their means. The workers of the exporting states were harnessed indirectly to feed this sloth and greed of the west; consumers felt no pain because the resulting hardships and despoilation were out of sight in foreign lands. It was a little like employing slaves, but keeping them in another country, rather than downstairs.

In this extraordinary period, money was conjured up from nowhere to feed the doomsday debt machine. Under the assumption that it was capable of infinite multiplication, money became unreal. Governments, whose role should be to assure the common good by protecting the people from the avarice of selfish individuals, colluded with businesses because of the huge taxation revenues that the moneymaking machine generated. Even the man in the street, in the developed economies at least, shared in the benefits and was far removed from the consequences.   Money had become the sole measure of a successful life, and people saw money and brilliance as synonymous. So it was easy to measure the value to society of a financier when the only measure was money – but how then were we to measure the contribution of a doctor, a teacher, a surgeon, nurse or scientist?

> …. a certain class of dishonesty, dishonesty magnificent in its proportions, and climbing into high places, has become at the same time so rampant and so splendid that men and women will be taught to feel that dishonesty, if it can become splendid, will cease to be abominable.[16]

If it was the strategy of the Chinese to replace the dollar with their own as the world's reserve currency, they failed. Downturn occurred in slow motion – death by a thousand cuts. First came the Global Financial Crisis of 2008. Then there was the Depression of 2014, followed two years later by the Crash of 2016, which tipped the world into a depression more severe than anything seen in modern times.

Depression in 2014

By 2011, the euro, a currency shared by the states of the European Union, had begun a slow decline caused by the excessive lending of the southern member states: The European Central Bank attempted to support the currency with its own debt, but failure was inevitable and the support was wasted. Greece ran out of money and withdrew from the shared currency in late 2013, followed in the same year by Ireland, Spain and Portugal, and Italy in 2014. The major European banks were one after another bankrupted by the failure of their sovereign loans; as each collapsed, it was taken over by the parent state and refinanced with yet *more* borrowed money. When Italy fell, the Euro

---

[16] Anthony Trollope, *The Way We Live Now*

collapsed. Northern Europe - Germany, the Benelux countries and the Scandinavian states - agreed to share the Neumark. France, deeply in debt herself and with her banks in ruins after so many sovereign defaults, reverted to the franc. The most indebted states, the USA, UK and France continued to print money, attempting to diminish the value of their currencies and debt.

In the years following the Global Financial Crisis of 2008, growth was weak or non-existent. Japan had already stagnated for over a decade. Now the whole of Europe succumbed to the 'Japanese Disease', at it came to be called. The depression of 2014 had begun. Australia survived 2008 intact and promptly embarked on a property boom, financed by easily borrowed money. When the depression began, it triggered a collapse of the overheated property market, and Australia experienced the first major banking collapse in its charmed history.

As depression bit, spending in importing countries diminished and Chinese exports fell. To stimulate their economy, the Chinese leadership fell back on the twelfth five-year plan, which had begun in 2010. The communist party had long hoped to improve wages and living conditions for their long-suffering people and had assumed that the money to finance the plan could be provided by selling down holdings of US dollar bonds; at first it succeeded, because, paradoxically, people with money sought safety from uncertainty in the haven of the US dollar. But with depression came reduced income tax revenue, and it became increasingly difficult for the USA to repay loans and interest to the holders of its bonds. Republican extremists in Congress refused to sanction further borrowing, or an increase in taxation proposed by a lame-duck president. All the rating agencies downgraded US Treasuries as it became clear that the USA was neither willing to pay the interest nor ever able to repay its borrowing.

The leaders of China found that there were no buyers for their US Treasury bonds, and learnt to their horror that they would never see their money again. The market panicked, a sell-off of bonds began, the USA finally defaulted and disaster struck.[17] In a chain reaction, banks across the world holding now valueless US bonds collapsed and depositors' funds were lost. US assets abroad, such as production licences, property, shares, bonds, ships and airplanes, were immediately sequestered. With no money to lend, banks were unable to support the bond markets of other heavily indebted countries, which in turn collapsed, and which triggered the further sequestration of foreign assets.

The Crash of 2016

Things only got worse. The resulting chain reaction swept across the world in one appalling week in February 2016. Interbank lending and international exchange, the system for interchangeability of currencies, ceased, and with it all foreign trade and investment stopped. Local real estate markets everywhere fell. The effect was to wipe clean the slate of the large borrowers: the USA, France, Brazil, the UK, India and others were relieved of their debt burdens. The lenders - China, Taiwan, Singapore, Germany and the Middle Eastern oil and gas states - were left with foreign assets that were worthless. Corporations which had invested billions to develop assets overseas, or in ventures aimed at export from home to abroad, found themselves owning worthless, stranded assets.

Stock exchanges buckled, taking pension schemes and investment income down with them. The retired found themselves thrown into poverty. Working people everywhere abandoned hope of a secure old age. Businesses, themselves bankrupt and with their

---

[17] What happens if the world's largest debtor defaults? Hamish McRae, *The Independent*, 29 July 2011

stockholders bankrupt, found themselves abandoned by their owners.

The international shipping of oil and gas was immediately suspended. Without fuel for transportation, food could not be harvested or distributed, and foreign workers and travellers were trapped away from home with no resources and no way to return. Ships were stranded in port, and aircraft on the ground. Telecommunications browned out.

Without imported fuel oil to generate electricity, drinking water could not be pumped nor sewage treated. As a result, many large cities, such as Karachi, Bangkok, Caracas, Cairo – even New York in the USA – became ungovernable. A massive exodus began, from every large city to rural areas; many people perished from thirst and hunger as they clogged transport arteries and motorways, attempting to flee into the surrounding countryside, deserts or jungles, while others barricaded themselves in their streets and tower blocks to escape the chaos of looting and theft.

Less affected were those who lived in rural areas and on the land, because they were closer to the sources of food and water supply. Poorer rural communities in the less developed countries were the least affected, because they were accustomed to self-sufficiency; family units were still strong in these areas, so their societies remained resilient and self-sufficient, taking care of the old, young and unwell, foraging, growing food and providing security. Conversely, in the developed western societies it was too often a case of 'every man for himself', and many of the weak, old and lonely were left for dead.

Much of industry at this time was adapted to the global market-place, and when transport stopped, so did the supply of feedstock, parts and materials, along with the market for completed goods and services. The practice of 'just in time' inventories meant there was no contingency for scrounging of alternatives. Activities such as banking, manufacture, mining, transport, tourism, and advertising were no longer essential. Unemployment in the private sector grew rapidly. More jobs were retained in the public services because they provided essential needs. The industries that survived the first days after the Crash were related to the supply of water, food, energy, medical treatment, pharmaceuticals, and building and construction. The employees of companies that were still viable, which still fulfilled a need or demand of society, kept going in to work; even where they were at first unpaid, they got on with their jobs, elected chief executives, reorganised themselves, and somehow managed to continue in business.

Poverty naturally followed the huge spike in unemployment. In Australia, many of the people who fled to the countryside lived in refugee camps on the outskirts of cities and towns, in shantytown communities. Their shelters resembled the riverbank humpies of black people, remembered, from their childhood, by many Australians of my generation. Some were even more wretched, existing in roadside encampments under scraps of fabric resembling the squalid hasty rehousing of Afghan refugees in Pakistan a decade earlier.

National governments became almost irrelevant. There were no longer any foreign affairs, trade or finance to be managed; the one exception was defence. Communities took control of their own lives and government. It was much like the aftermath of the 2011 tsunami in Japan, where local communities had been seen demonstrating hidden depths of resourcefulness in the face of the inaction of a shallow and corrupt central government. Communities in nations such as France, in which much power was already devolved to local communes, had a head start. In Australia, the six state parliaments, which some had thought to be redundant, suddenly found a renewed purpose; on the other hand, Australians soon came to regret the abolition of the many town and shire councils established well over one hundred years before.

The strength of government institutions was tested to its end limits; where the chaos was greatest, complete breakdown occurred. States of emergency were declared and military takeovers became commonplace. In India, this succeeded in stabilising the union; in Pakistan, military leadership hardened but with the public purse empty, the armed forces abandoned Baluchistan and the Pashtun region to gang rule and a reversion to tribalism.

The need for security was greater than ever. Warfare for ideology was supplanted by war for survival. Military forces were dispersed to support local government and law and order, or were deployed to borders to block, by force, the influx of refugees. With the breakdown of the financial sector, some armies were forced to forage in their community for survival. Bloody battles and massacres occurred at many borders, to prevent refugees from swamping the resources of the state, region or tribe. The US, desperate for imported energy, ordered the defence forces to colonise the oil production systems of the Middle East and, under the protection of the US navy, shuttled oil tankers back and forth across the Atlantic.

With its huge debt repudiated, Chinese export income ceased as trade ended; without trade, there were neither the imported raw materials nor markets for manufacturing. Local markets for their huge production capability did not exist, so layoffs of Chinese labour were huge. Unemployment snowballed, triggering violent urban uprisings and rural poverty. With personal incomes slashed, the real-estate market fell. The mighty People's Republic once again descended into warlordism and anarchy. In the boom years, we had forgotten China's potential for chaos and destruction, which is why we found its precipitate collapse so surprising.

The great survivors of this period were countries of what can be called 'genius', like France, Sweden, Taiwan, Brazil and Germany. They had wisely preserved their own agriculture, resources of energy and industrial capacity; other, isolated, island-like states, such as Australia and South Africa, survived because they had retained their economic self-sufficiency in the face of globalisation. Hardest hit were those in which chaos, revolution and anarchy had never been far from the surface.

A new world order emerges

Gradually, in the decade following the Crash of 2016, order was restored across the world. Agriculture adapted quickly to provide self-sufficiency in food; old waste-disposal sites were reopened and mined for raw materials. Energy crops producing ethanol and biodiesel oil were soon substituted for imported oil, and road, sea and even some air transport was reinstated. Self-sufficiency in energy was vital for survival. France, with 85% of her power derived from nuclear generation, and Switzerland and Sweden, with approximately 50% hydro and 40% nuclear capacity respectively, hardly faltered.

States such as Singapore and Hong Kong, with vigorous populations but insufficient land for agriculture, were compelled to expropriate an area of mainland capable of feeding their populations. Thus, Singapore annexed Johore Bahru from Malaysia, and Hong Kong took control of much of the province of Guangdong from the fragmenting People's Republic. In Australia and many other countries, manufacturing industries, which had largely withered away through competition from China in items such as clothing, footwear, household goods and building materials, were rebuilt. Country towns and cities, only recently depopulated by the drift to the cities, were repopulated.

No one will ever know precisely how many people lost their lives in this period of chaos, but it was at least an order of magnitude greater than the depredations of Mao Tse Tung. Worldwide estimates range between one and two billion. Tragic as this was at the time, however, this appalling toll was a mere prologue to the approaching disaster of climate change.

Too many people?

Some historians have blamed over-exploitation of the world's resources on the excesses of neo-liberal capitalism, the greed of the financial industry and its seduction of governments. I believe that the ultimate root cause of the exhaustion of the atmosphere, agriculture, and energy and water resources was the uncontrolled growth of the world's population.

> There is no exception to the rule that every organic being naturally increases at so high a rate, that, if not destroyed, the earth would soon be covered by the progeny of a single pair. Even slow-breeding man has doubled in twenty-five years, and at this rate, in less than a thousand years, there would literally not be standing room for his progeny.[18]

In prehistory, mankind struggled to survive. For millennia, the population of the Earth oscillated between two levels of equilibrium. During each interglacial, population increased to an upper limit, and then reduced to a lower limit during each glacial period, owing to the harsh environment and high death rate. But by the first decades of the twenty-first century, advances in civil engineering had improved the quality of drinking water and sanitation, eliminating many diseases and improving public health. Breakthroughs in medicine, particularly the use of

---

[18] Charles Darwin, *Origin of the Species*

inoculation to create immunity to disease, had extended life expectancy; mechanised agriculture, fertilisers, pesticides and irrigation had increased the supply of food. Gradually, restraints on population growth were removed, while the drive to procreate endured, fed by hard-wired sexual drive and cultural-religious norms.

As a cancer grows without restraint, to ultimately destroy the host that gives it life, so did we. Why? When we look at nature, we see stable, complex organisms and communities that limit their size in order to survive. At a more complex level, the early aboriginal settlers of Australia devised a social system in which communities controlled their size in order to harmonize and co-exist with the rest of life.

Until the Crash of 2016, there were very few people with the courage to talk about population. It was as if it was taboo to question the implicit assumption that the right to procreate was a most fundamental human right. Even as the world's population passed seven billions in 2012 and the availability of agricultural land reached its upper limit, we spoke about the need to increase food yields and available land. China made a half-hearted attempt to halt population growth, but quietly abandoned it on discovery of the benefits of growth and neoliberal capitalism. Thinkers such as the naturalist and broadcaster David Attenborough quietly, yet firmly put forward the case for restraint. Unfortunately, they were not heard.

The right way lost

And so, an era in which great centralised governments, centralised multinational corporations and globalisation had risen to prominence, drew to a close; these institutions had brought short-term material wealth to the world, but, in the long term, nothing but misery. They had failed society and had to be discarded.

Future generations had been robbed of energy, vast quantities of carbon laid down over millennia having been consumed with no thought for the future. We, as the doorkeepers of the treasury of our children, had borrowed money from the future, impoverishing them, incurring huge government and business debts, speculating with the value of businesses and property, and deferring the cost of enormous pension commitments. We had, in a word, failed. The great irony now in 2053, is that a powerful and robust civilisation, such as Australia, which had obliterated a fragile 60,000-year-old aboriginal society, had endured for just another two hundred years before destroying itself as well.

Reeling from the Crash, humanity faced the inexorable and encroaching menace of climate change, impoverished, ill prepared and sunk in global depression; it faced the greatest challenge to its existence since the Toba bottleneck 73,000 years before. Resources which could have been invested in preparations for fundamental change had been misdirected, squandered in the pursuit of endless growth, unnecessary warfare and the generation of more money.

In short, we were lost. The next chapter will consider how the lessons of the Crash pointed the way ahead for the journey into the dark decades of climate change and the unforeseen direction which the world was to take.

THREE

The darkest hour

There is a beautiful saying with which the Irish inspire hope under adverse circumstances: Remember, they say, that the darkest hour of all is the hour before day.[19]

One million people died in the Irish famine of 1845-1852, and many more migrated, so that in the forty years between the censuses of 1841 and 1881, the country's population fell from 8.2 to 5.2 million, or by almost 40%. The deaths were due to a collapse in food production brought about by mismanagement of the land by out-of-touch, absentee English landlords, after enclosure of the common lands. Now, these tragic figures seem puny compared to the losses of the last decades. In the closing days of the twentieth century, they were a forgotten backwater of history. History was destined to repeat itself.

The depression that the world had to have

This chapter will look back on the end of growth, then on how the world responded to the challenge of depression; for some it led to destruction, for others to rebirth. It will also trace the surprising and unexpected path of climate change, the destruction it wrought, and the unbelievable folly of our species. How is it that we could know of similar events in our history, and yet fail to see the signs of own impending doom and act to avert it. The Earth got to where we are largely by chance, by surrendering to 'events', rather than through any conscious act or intention.

---

[19] Samuel Lover, *Songs and Ballads*

In the years following the Crash of 2016, the world slumped into a dark decade of economic depression more severe than any experienced since the Black Death – the series of plagues which decimated Europe in the Middle Ages.[20]

With depression, economic growth ended, for ever. The havoc of economic depression was a precursor of the far greater hardship and stress to be wrought by climate change. It takes stress to drive innovation and diversity, and it takes hardship to select the fittest adaptations. For those incapable of change, it was the first of a series of increasingly savage blows; for the adaptable, it served as a call to action and innovation. This was a critical call to humankind to mobilise every available resource to fight the approaching battle for survival. So, although it was a period of economic stagnation and shrinkage, mankind began the process of change that would allow it to overcome the far greater threat of climate change lurking in ambush in the decades ahead.

I contend that this was the depression that the world had to have! The logic of free market capitalism had always been that economic growth must continue if we were to avoid collapse and depression. Our governments needed growth to feed the public debts they created to feed our insatiable desire for more handouts, subsidies, overseas military adventures and public services. We ourselves needed more money to buy ever more expensive houses, to afford manufactured goods and to support employment for our children as they entered the workforce.

The end of growth

It is true that we foresaw the need to restrict growth, but when it came to action, the developed countries were too prosperous, fat, complacent, and selfish to act in an altruistic way; the developing countries were too preoccupied by the inequity of their situation,

---

[20] Barbara Tuchman, *A Distant Mirror*

too intent on aspiring to the prosperity of the developed world, to stop their acquisitive drive. If, in 2012, all seven billion people on the planet had consumed as much as the average American, we would have required the resources of four planets; we would have needed two planets if everyone had consumed as much as the average European. We really thought that the whole great machine could go on for ever. How could we ever have thought so? Thomas Malthus, writing in 1798, gloomily observed:

> The power of population is so superior to the power of the earth to produce subsistence for man, that premature death must in some shape or other visit the human race.[21]

John Stuart Mill reiterated the question in 1848:

> Towards what ultimate point is society tending by its industrial progress? When the progress ceases, in what condition are we to expect that it will leave mankind? ...

> If the earth must lose that great proportion of its pleasantness which it owes to things that the unlimited increase in wealth and population would extirpate from it, for the mere purpose of enabling it to support a larger, but not a better or a happier population, I sincerely hope, for the sake of posterity, that they will be content to be stationary, long before necessity compels them to it.[22]

The 'Limits to Growth', first published in 1972 by the Club of Rome, described a seminal attempt to model the consequences, for

---

[21] T. R. Malthus, *An Essay on the Principle of Population*

[22] J. S. Mill, *Principles of Political Economy with some of their Applications to Social Philosophy*

a rapidly growing world, of limits on the supply of resources. This brilliant work was subsequently ignored on the grounds that it was oversimplified and constituted a doomsday prophecy that had not held up to scrutiny.

The conventional wisdom was that only growth could pull people out of poverty and remove the inequitable allocation of wealth across the world. Governments sought economic expansion to assure growth in their spending ability and hence their capability for change, or at least the implementation of their policies. However, as Malthus and Mill had observed, the opposite was the case: the inescapable logic was that we could achieve equity only by the rich consuming less and by there being less of us on the planet. The exponential growth of money had overshot the capability of the planet to sustain it. A huge unanswered question hung before us: what would we live for if we did not live for money?

What have I got to live for?

The way goods and services were priced in the economy in the decades leading up to the Crash did not reflect how the economy interacted with the environment. The things we took from the environment, and the things we returned to the environment were ignored and not priced in monetary terms, despite their incalculable value and importance, not just to our well being, but to our survival. An economy is not a perpetual motion machine, but must take account of the one-way entropic input of matter and energy. The dilemma was that the impact of recognising sustainability was so great that no democratically elected government had the courage to entertain it.

Our economic and social systems connoted growth with an increase in well-being. There was once a time when money was indispensable for happiness – to assure our physiological needs such as food and water, to assure safety of employment, a home to live in, to support and raise a family and to pay our dues to the society which nurtured us. But as wealth increased, money began to be used to boost self-esteem, and as a way of comparing our success, in both the personal and the public arena; we turned it into a measure of happiness and accomplishment – a measure of all things. So, instead of respecting values that could guide us through life, such as generosity, beauty, learning, wisdom, thoughtfulness, creativity, conversation, sporting achievement, musical ability and family stability, we respected fast cars, expensive houses, the size of our salary or bonus. Most pernicious of all was the miasma of advertising that enveloped us, telling us that we would be happy, beautiful, successful, if we bought something we really didn't need. Our so-called 'basic needs' had assumed gargantuan proportions. However, beyond these 'basic needs', money brought us many ills as well: stress, congestion, anxiety, depression, overwork, noise, pollution, illness and sleeplessness.

Expensive holidays were meant to compensate for the leisure lost though overwork and lack of time. We had to buy gourmet fast foods because we did not have time to shop and cook properly. Costly gyms and running machines were purchased because we had nowhere to exercise in the urban jungle. We provided our children with flat-screen televisions and electronic games to occupy them because we did not have time to teach and relax with them. Looking after ourselves properly became more expensive through warranted and sometimes unwarranted medical care. Time, or the lack of it, had become a curse.

And why didn't we have time? That was because we spent hours every day burning petrol in a motorcar that was unnecessarily large, driving from our mortgaged home to work in a large centralised office or factory.

This was the great unspeakable truth of the age before the Crash: that continuous growth, of population and of money, was unsustainable and impossible.

Blind to the future

The dialogue before the Crash of 2016 was long on descriptions of owhat was happening to the planet, but short on suggested actions and effective responses. There was significant scepticism about 'the science', as if the science was separable from all the other aspects of climate change. I believe now that the professions of science, too specialised and constrained by their ethic of proof-by- experiment, were not robust enough in promoting their thinking. Science and medicine had lost sight of the big picture, and there were too few synthesisers, multi-disciplinary thinkers, as Schrödinger once observed:

> ... it has become next to impossible for a single mind fully to command more than a small specialized portion of it [i.e. knowledge]. I can see no other escape from this dilemma (lest our true aim be lost forever) than that some of us should venture to embark on a synthesis of facts and theories, albeit with second-hand and incomplete knowledge of some of them, and at the risk of making fools of ourselves.[23]

The economics profession, which should also have spoken up, had become apologists for the mountebanks of finance. Nicholas Stern even tried to evaluate the value of the whole world in monetary terms. He later conceded the difficulty of this approach, admitting that ...

> Looking back, I underestimated the risks. The planet and the atmosphere seem to be absorbing less carbon than we expected, and

---

[23] Erwin Schrödinger, *What is Life? The Physical Aspect of the Living Cell*, lectures delivered in Dublin 1943

emissions are rising pretty strongly. Some of the effects are coming through more quickly than we thought then....

This is potentially so dangerous that we have to act strongly. Do we want to play Russian roulette with two bullets or one? These risks for many people are existential.[24]

A succession of high-profile international climate-change conferences were hampered by national rivalries and the risks to incumbent governments of putting forward painful policies in a democratic society. It took the Crash to generate a 'critical mass' of public opinion in favour of change, to begin serious discussions and evaluation of practical measures that could be taken to avert or respond to climate change.

Great, insightful work, often sponsored by governments, was at first ignored. The Sustainable Development Commission in the UK, for instance, published 'Prosperity Without Growth' in March 2009, addressing the concepts of prosperity, well being and happiness in a steady-state economy. It considered the kind of economics that would maintain economic stability without growth; amazingly, almost no one had attempted this. Another of the lone voices was Canadian economist Peter Victor, one of the very few who attempted at this time to describe a no-growth economy.

It was becoming clear that, to respond to the challenge of climate change, we were going to have to reconsider the options to population and money growth – fundamentally, what constituted happiness, what were the minimum requirements for happiness, and what we were going to do about it. For an individual, the choices were possibly quite simple, but, collectively, for seven billion people, these were impossible questions to answer.

---

[24] Nicholas Stern, interviewed in *The Observer*, 26 January 2013

Self-interest was too embedded to be able to avert the 'tragedy of the commons'. Nature managed the outcome for us:

> All for ourselves and nothing for other people seems, in every age of the world, to have been the vile maxim of the masters of mankind.[25]

The Crash of 2016 led to a spectrum of outcomes, from the tragic to the heroic. Every society responded in its own way, and those that survived now have their own stories to tell. Let us consider, in particular, the case of Australia. At the time of the Crash, Australia found itself well off, but with a prosperity dependent on exports of raw materials to the growing economies of Asia. The Australian people, in the decades before the federation of the colonies in 1901, and in the two world wars, had displayed altruism and strength to an unusual degree, but by 2016 these qualities had become dormant; prosperity had bred complacency, governments had become mediocre, managerialism had supplanted leadership, vested interests dominated the country's public life, and the people did not care.

The aftermath of 2016, particularly the disappearance of international trade, highlighted the absence of consensus within Australia on a national strategy for climate change. It was no longer possible to lay back and trust in the Lucky Country. Climate change would continue remorselessly, and the whole world was now aware of the new economic and commercial realities. It was at this time that my small book, *Australia Phoenix: 2053* became a national bestseller and added another small voice to the clamour that awoke the country to its destiny as a lifeboat for humanity.

---

[25] Adam Smith, *The Wealth of Nations*.

The idea that it was too late to respond meaningfully to climate change had been put forward by James Lovelock[26] in 2009:

> Because of the rapidity of the Earth's change we will need to respond more like the inhabitants of a city threatened by a flood. When they see the unstoppable rise of water, their only option is to escape to higher ground; it is too late for them to do anything else, as it is for us to try to save our familiar world .... Keep in mind that it is hubris to think that we know how to save the Earth: our planet looks after itself. All that we can do is try to save ourselves.

There was a time when we humans thought that we could push the Earth's systems a bit, looking forward to finally gaining control over carbon dioxide production, so we could let the system rebound to where we began. Now we realised that change was unstoppable, already in motion, like a runaway train. Climate events after 2016 rapidly worsened across the globe. Too late we understood that the system was neither linear nor controllable, that it could rapidly fall into new, unexpected, unpredictable states of equilibrium, from which there was no turning back except over centuries or millennia.

More of the same, only worse

In the first years, the severity and frequency of natural disasters increased – namely, flood, drought, earthquake, tsunami, hurricane, fire and epidemic disease. Locations and damage were predictable extrapolations of what had gone before: the hurricane which flattened Houston, Galveston and Texas City, the earthquake which brought havoc to north-western China, the tsunami which devastated Tokyo and Yokahama, the fire which burned almost half of the Amazon forest in one dry summer, or the floods which scoured the Ganges Valley from the Himalayan foothills to Bangladesh.

---

[26] James Lovelock, *The Vanishing Face of Gaia – A Final Warning*

Australia suffered grievously with increased occurrences of bush fires and flooding.

Crowding of people into cities and slums exacerbated the transmission of contagious diseases. Already by 2010, more than 30 million people in Africa were living with HIV, and 2 million died each year of the disease. In the northern spring of 2019, swine flu broke out in Mexico and soon spread across the world. The first wave caused some deaths in Mexico, but few elsewhere. However during the summer and autumn of that year, the virus evolved into a fierce, highly contagious strain, which swept the world during the following winter. It was estimated that one in every three people on the planet was sickened, and the loss of life, although never accurately counted, amounted to several hundred million. Anti-viral drugs and immunization were effective when used, but were available only in those nations whose governments had been farsighted enough to urgently prepare for the risk.

A similar but somewhat less severe epidemic of avian flu arose in northern China. This epidemic swept the world in 2021, before the threat of flu was neutralised by the release, in the USA, of an antisense DNA treatment which prevented viral replication.

Forest fires destroyed much of Amazonia in 2019; rainforest clearing had continued at such a ruthless pace that, by the southern summer of 2018, the rains, which had made that great river's catchment the lungs of the world, faltered and declined. Forest undergrowth, many metres deep in peat, began to dry and shrink, and peat fires, ignited by summer lightning storms, smouldered through the winter, only to reignite the following summer. So much smoke was produced that it spread across the Atlantic Ocean and formed a haze along the west coast of southern Africa. Destruction was many times more severe than the great Asian rainforest fires of the early 1990s, and the reduction of average temperature in Africa was immediate.

In the following winter of 2020, the Arctic Ocean did not freeze. Without its reflective white ice cap, the polar sea warmed as it absorbed heat from the summer sun. Melting rates of the Greenland glaciers set new records. Between 2003 and 2010, the Gravity Recovery and Climate Experiment had measured ice loss of 4,100 km^3 and sea level increase of 12 mm, or 1.6 mm each year[27] and each year following 2010 saw an increase in that melt rate. In 2022, the Icelandic ice cap, which at the turn of the century contained some 3,800 km^3 of frozen water, collapsed in a matter of weeks. Glacial-lake outburst flooding had been seen before, but never of this magnitude in recorded human history. Sea levels rose by 10 mm around the world. The flush of lower density fresh water into the North Atlantic Ocean further slowed the gulfstream conveyor current. Known as the Thermohaline Circulation, this current warmed western Europe; northern France, Ireland and the United Kingdom, which had previously enjoyed temperate climates, began to experience winters of Scandinavian intensity.

Flying too close to the sun

As living space became scarcer, people had been forced to live in harm's way. Uncontrolled population growth had consumed all the reserves of safe land, so that people had to live or farm in climatically or geologically ever more risky places, such as river valleys, coastal foreshores and river deltas, on low-lying islands and in areas that were seismically active. To these natural risks, we added man-made risks by building major dams upstream of

---

[27] http://www.colorado.edu/news/releases/2012/02/08/cu-boulder-study-shows-global-glaciers-ice-caps-shedding-billions-tons-mass

great cities, and nuclear power stations and chemical plants too close to populated areas. As the more readily producible mineral, oil and gas resources were exhausted, we were compelled to exploit more remote and hazardous reserves. The implications for mankind of these increased risks is illustrated by three incidents: in Abu Dhabi, Pakistan and the USA.

Abu Dhabi, the near bankrupt emirate, having produced all the readily accessible oil and gas in its territory, developed in desperation the Shah sour-gas field 140 km to the south of its settled coast. This was so risky a decision that only Royal Dutch Shell was rash enough to partner the national gas company in the project. Of the billion cubic feet per day of raw gas produced, 23% was hydrogen sulphide, a broad spectrum poison comparable in toxicity to hydrogen cyanide. At a concentration of 800 parts per million, it kills 50% of humans in 5 minutes. At 1,000 parts per million (0.1%), it kills after a single breath. It is also heavier than air. A previous accidental blow out of a sour-gas well in China in 2003 had killed 243 people and forced 9,000 to seek treatment. Hydrogen sulphide is a seriously dangerous substance which should have remained safely underground.

The gas was processed to make it safe for use by removing the hydrogen sulphide, which was then converted to the inert form of pure sulphur, at the rate of 10,000 tonne per day. The clean gas was exported, but there was no market for the sulphur, so it was stockpiled in the desert, millions of tons of it, in yellow brick mountains. Although 23% was the average content, gas from one well contained 43% of hydrogen sulphide. Late on a summer night in 2019, a foreign worker driving a mobile crane inadvertently backed into the wellhead, dislodging it from the well-casing and damaging the well's control equipment. Sadly, the down-hole safety valve had never been maintained, such was the health risk of working over this well, and so it failed. A plume of toxic gas, hugging the desert floor, was carried by the wind off the land directly over Abu Dhabi City. Confusion reigned all night and it was only at daylight that a Saudi fighter aircraft was scrambled to ignite the well with rocket fire. The population of the city died in their sleep; the city was left a ghost town, and still stands almost empty, a modern Pompeii.

Very few people know that, some ten years later, the Australian Navy contemplated an audacious expedition to set fire to the 15 million tonne stockpile of sulphur in Abu Dhabi. The object of the mission would have been to inject sulphur dioxide into the stratosphere to form a sol of sulphuric acid, which it was hoped would cool the Earth. The eruption of Mt Pinatubo in the Philippines in 1991 had injected 20 million tonne of sulphur dioxide into the atmosphere, halting atmospheric global warming for three years. Nature took its own course before the plan could be implemented.

In the year following the Abu Dhabi accident, disaster struck in Pakistan. The safety of large dams has been a perennial concern of engineers, and Pakistan had its share of such facilities, with Tarbela Dam on the mighty Indus River and Mangla on the Jhelum. The UNEP (United Nations Environment Program) had warned repeatedly of the risk of glacier-lake outburst floods in the Himalaya and Karakoram Ranges.[28] In 1841, a rubble dam, created by a landslide which had blocked the Indus at Raikot-Astor, broke, causing a 25 m high flood as far downstream as Attock, with a flowrate estimated at 540,000 cumecs (cubic metres per second).[29] [30] To put this in perspective, the overflow capacity

---

[28] http://www.grida.no/publications/high-mountain-glaciers
[29] Indus Floods and Syok Glaciers, *Himalayan Journal*, Keneth Mason (1929), http://www.himalayanclub.org/journal/indus-floods-and-shyok-glaciers/
[30] The World's Largest Floods, Past and Present: Their Causes and Magnitudes, *US Geological Survey*, http://pubs.usgs.gov/circ/2004/circ1254/pdf/circ1254.pdf

of the modern Tarbela Dam, just upstream from Attock, was 18,406 cumecs over the main spillway and 24,070 cumecs over the auxiliary spillway. Maximum capacity of the dam was 14.3 km³. By 2020, more than half of this capacity had been taken up by silt, because the river dumped 430 million tonne of silt per year into the dam. Up to that time, the world's worst recorded landslide dam-outburst disaster had occurred in 1786 on the Dadu River in Sichuan in China, in which a flood extended downstream 1400 km, drowning an estimated 100,000 people.[31]

In 2010, a huge landslide had blocked the Hunza River, a tributary of the Indus, at Attaabad. Half-hearted attempts were made to construct a spillway to reduce water level, but complacency grew with time, and successively weaker governments in Islamabad procrastinated on any action which would relieve the danger. With time the emergency was forgotten. As glacial melt increased with global warming, previously frozen terrain thawed and landslips became more prevalent. In 2020, a smaller lake upstream of Hunza failed and overtopped another slightly larger lake downstream; the resulting flood wave overwhelmed the makeshift spillway of the Hunza Lake and the whole unstable mass of rubble collapsed catastrophically. The lake emptied in minutes, sending a wave of water downstream. Twelve hours later, the flood wave overwhelmed Tarbela's spillways, the 148 m high earth and rockfill dam was overtopped and breached, releasing the impounded water and silt.

Half the population of this crowded country lost their lives in the ensuing flood, which swept downstream to Karachi, destroying

---

[31] S G Evans, THE FORMATION AND FAILURE OF LANDSLIDE DAMS: AN APPROACH TO RISK ASSESSMENT http://www.ijege.uniroma1.it/rivista/special-2006/special-2006/the-formation-and-failure-of-landslide-dams-an-approach-to-risk-assessment/ijege-special-06-evans.pdf

the irrigation barrages as it went, releasing yet more water. The final knockout blow was the localised earthquake which demolished Islamabad-Rawalpindi, triggered by the sudden removal of the weight of 10 km^3 of water and silt from a point on the Earth's crust 50 km distant. With its irrigated breadbasket gone and central government immobilised, the survivors welcomed humanitarian aid from India and in the following year chose by referendum to join the Indian union.

This catastrophe, in the longer term, called into question the viability of all large dam projects downstream of melting glacial regions. On the Ganges, Mekong and Yangtze Rivers, there were already many large dams and more were in construction. Projects already troubled by the financial turmoil were paralysed by safety assessments and redesign. In China, where the Three Gorges Dam had always been controversial, the government decided, after further risk assessment, to operate the dam at 75% of capacity; electric power output was little changed, but irrigation and food production were sacrificed. As central control over the allocation of irrigation water weakened, famine returned to India and China. The starving trekked to where they hoped they could survive, to either ravage all before them or to be forcefully excluded by the existing population, whose first thought was to preserve their own lives. Internal migration to seek water became widespread across the world, inevitably leading to civil violence.

By far the most devastating of all natural disasters of this time was the tsunami which engulfed the eastern seaboard of the United States. Seismic activity around the Canary Island of El Hierro kindled in 2011, and gradually increased in severity. In 2014, a sixth volcanic island emerged from the Atlantic and continued to grow in size. In 2022, the western flank of the island of Cumbre Vieja, gradually weakened by ground displacement and motion, subsided into the Atlantic Ocean. The slip occurred only one month after the Icelandic sea level rise of 10 mm, so soon that geologists suspect the very slight increase in water pressure was the final straw which upset the equilibrium of forces and triggered the collapse. Underwater, 500 km^3 of rock slid to the ocean floor, generating a mega-tsunami that eventually impinged on the whole coastline of the ocean. Nowhere was the damage as great as the eastern seaboard of the USA, where many major coastal cities were obliterated and in some places the wave ran up as far as the Appalachian Mountains. The great coastal cities of South America were similarly inundated, and seawater swept over the Amazon delta, penetrating many hundreds of kilometres inland. All the coastal seaports and waterways, all the shipping which lay in harbours along the coast, including one third of the US Navy's ships, were destroyed. Nothing was left of Washington, so the federal capital was re-established in Atlanta.

Global cooling – a new ice age

All the while, the Earth steadily warmed. After 2016, the consumption of hydrocarbons reduced dramatically, owing to austerity and reduced industrial activity. The concentration of carbon dioxide in the atmosphere had stopped increasing; some even dared to hope that it would begin to fall, if we could only develop nuclear capacity quickly enough. Then things took an unexpected turn. The world quickly became very much colder. We were caught by surprise; once again, we had ignored what natural history and geology had told us had occurred many times in the past.

The Earth's crust is formed of large rafts of solid rock called tectonic plates, which float on the underlying fluid of molten rock. Where the rafts bump into each other, one edge slides under the other; earthquakes are prevalent. Where the plates are separating, molten rock wells up, often as volcanoes, to fill the gaps. The plates are carried slowly across the Earth's surface by convection currents in the fluid rock, driven by the heat from deep below. At each pole, the plates are sunk deeper by the huge weight of water frozen in the icecaps above; in 2011, the Greenland icecap, for instance, was estimated to contain 2.9 million km^3 of ice and Iceland to support 3,800 km^3 of ice. When the weight of the ice on a plate is reduced, it rises up, and when ice weight is added, the raft sinks into the fluid. However, it is more complicated than that, because the fluid is partly plastic and the raft is elastic. When an area of ice melts, the floating raft rises at the point of weight removal by bending up, but the surrounding raft sinks to compensate. It is a slow process; land in the area of Hudson Bay, for instance, was still rising at a rate of 10 mm/yr in 2005, owing to the melting of an ice cap 15,000 years earlier. Eventually, everything levels out again, but while it does, the plate is flexing. This phenomenon is called 'elasto-plastic rebound' and has happened a lot at the poles of the planet as ice caps have come and gone. With all this movement, it is no accident that two of the weakest spots in the Earths crust, and the most prone to large volcanoes, lie near the poles: Iceland and Tierra del Fuego, the 'land of fire'.

Analysis of cores drilled from the ice in both Antarctica and Greenland has enabled calculation of global average temperature and volcanicity, going back 110,000 years. Volcanicity was determined by measurement of dust, and temperature by measurement of the ratio of oxygen isotopes ^{16}O and ^{18}O in water. Comparison of the two data sets demonstrated a strong correlation between volcanic events and the onset of millennial cold periods. The clear conclusion was that ice-sheet unloading and sea level rise correlated with increased volcanism during the Wurm and Holocene. In other words, ice-sheet melting due to atmospheric heating resulted in elasto-plastic flexure, which, by over-stressing the Earth's crust, had released volcanoes in the past at the Iceland and Tierra del Fuego tectonic hot spots.[32]

And this is exactly what happened in 2031. In the north, the Icelandic cap had completely melted by 2022 and the Greenland icecap continued to melt at an alarming rate. Localised earth tremors were becoming more frequent as the icecap weight reduced. In the late summer of 2031, the glacial outburst of a huge lake deep under the ice released 400 km³ of water into the Arctic Ocean in the space of a few days. This single incident raised the level of the ocean by a minuscule 1 mm, but created a sufficient increase in the buoyancy of other glacier tongues entering the sea to release further water outbursts in Greenland and West Antarctica. More substantial earth tremors followed, rocking Iceland, which within weeks was obliterated by the huge explosive eruption of Oyefjelljokelen. Within six months, at the other pole, triggered by more summer melting in West Antarctica, volcanoes in the extreme south of Chile also came to life. Over a period of eight months, so much sulphur dioxide and ash was pumped into the stratosphere that the planet cooled by 3 C.[33]

Tragically, the further increase in sea level triggered disaster on the western seaboard of the United States. The movement of tectonic plate edges at the north and south polar hot spots unzipped inbuilt stresses along plate edges all the way to the equator. The San Andreas Fault, which had been monitored with

---

[32] For a comprehensive summary of the many possible scenarios, refer to: B. McGuire, *Potential for a hazardous geospheric response to projected future climate changes*, Phil. Trans. R. Soc. A 28 May 2010 vol. 368 no. 1919

[33] Mini ice age took hold of Europe in months, *New Scientist*, 11 November 2009, describing work reported by William Patterson of the University of Saskatchewan on the study of mud cores from Lough Monreagh in Ireland, which shows that the Younger Dryas mini ice age, which began around 12,800 years ago, engulfed Europe in just months.

concern for decades, finally gave way, releasing so much energy that in California, a Richter magnitude of 10.1 was observed, the largest measurement ever recorded of an earthquake, exceeding the 9.5 measured in Chile in 1960. With first its east coast and now the west destroyed, the USA turned further inwards, a much-diminished nation, although it remains to this day the world's largest national economy.

Looking back in sadness

Even now, it astonishes me that these events were not anticipated more widely. Each and every one of the major events occurring in Abu Dhabi, Pakistan and the USA had been subject to monitoring and analysis for decades. Scientists had been issuing regular warnings on each one, but the world had deaf ears. It shows us how debased our political leadership had become that they failed to heed the warnings and to provide for the security of their citizens.

In 2031, winter began early in Europe, and summer the following year was almost indiscernible. The effect on Russia, Scandinavia and Canada was severe, and occurred in a space of weeks after the first eruptions. Intense frosts and snowfall crippled travel, food and water supply. Whole cities in the northern regions were frozen and remain inaccessible to this day under a growing blanket of ice. The latitude delimiting all-year-round snow cover moved south by some 1000 km; now, inland Norway, Finland and Sweden no longer thaw in summer and the Baltic remains frozen all year round. Following a year without summer, the north of Germany, France and the USA began to experience shorter, cooler summers, and their climate has remained colder.

Australia, in the middle latitudes of the southern hemisphere, now enjoys a milder, wetter climate. The desert interior is well watered, Lake Eyre full, and the Murray River once again flows into the sea throughout the year.

The volcanoes have gradually become extinguished, but the world remains frozen in a new glacial. The huge increase in area of reflective snow and ice in the high latitudes, combined with a gradual downward trend in carbon dioxide concentration, has ended the benign interglacial period and settled the Earth into a new equilibrium state, the Anthropocene Glaciation. Global population has reduced to one billion. Like Europe after the Black Death of the fourteenth century, vast regions now remain fallow and are returning to nature.

That is the story of how by over-exploiting the commons which was our beautiful planet, we caused indescribable horror and anguish for so many and took mankind to the brink of destruction. It is a story of short-sightedness, selfishness, ignorance, folly and arrogance. I have told it again because it must go down in our annals and never be forgotten. It must inform the future actions of our species so that we forever collaborate with nature and live in harmony with the world.

In the final three chapters, I would like to reflect on the way we are now; how the survivors are adapting to the new realities, how fortune has once more blessed Australia, and the formidable challenges that still lie ahead of us. It is a story of rebirth, a new renaissance.

FOUR

A lifeboat

lifeboat n. a boat used for rescuing people at sea, escaping from a sinking ship, etc

Looking back now, thirty seven years after the Crash of 2016, it still amazes me that certain nations, Australia among them, were able to surmount global economic exhaustion and prepare for climate change. To some extent, its survival was due to luck – Australia Felix, the Lucky Country once again, blessed with its isolated setting in the mid-latitudes of the southern hemisphere; but it was also due to the wise preparation of what we called a 'lifeboat', capable of rescue and the means of escape to a new beginning.

The least of all possible evils

This most recent survival was a very close-run 'achievement'. The onslaught of the Anthropocene glacial over the last few decades, although a great disaster for mankind, represents the least of many possible evils that could have beset the Earth; if global heating had continued, we could very well have driven the Earth into a new Eocene-like period[34] in which the planet would have become very hot, and most life, including our species, would have perished. The Eocene was a recent event in geological time, occurring 56 to 34 million years ago, not long ago when you consider that the Earth is 3,400 million years old. This is what

---

[34] Arctic meltdown is a threat to humanity, Fred Pearce, *New Scientist*, 25 March 2009

would have happened if the arctic permafrost and the vast deposits of hydrated methane on the ocean floors had melted before the Greenland and West Antarctic ice caps collapsed. Methane is a much more potent greenhouse gas than carbon dioxide, with the potential for much greater heating.

The double blow to the world's population of, first, the Crash of 2016 and then global cooling, was profound. Total population is now, in 2053, estimated to be one billion, down from a maximum of over seven billion. We will never know the exact figure, because anarchy, still widespread in many surviving regions, prevents accurate gathering of the data. Australia has had its share of death and destruction, but has been fortunate compared to most; the country's population now stands at 20 million, down some 12% from its peak in 2015.

Who survived?

Where has life been preserved, where has civil society endured, and why? All those societies that have survived have done so through their fortuitous geographical position. Countries in equatorial and mid-latitudes have been favoured, as glaciation pushed climate systems towards the equator. Areas of desert have moved with them, bringing regular rainfall to land previously desert, and turning once-fertile areas to wilderness. Many islands have been spared, among them Japan, Taiwan, New Zealand, Ireland, the United Kingdom, Indonesia, the Philippines, Sri Lanka, peninsular Spain and Australia, owing to their temperate climates or their protective moats of sea warmed by ocean currents.

Some people have also survived in mountain enclaves in Turkey, South America, and in many small communities across Asia and Africa, but in disorganised, nearly tribal conditions, living in a primitive way and pillaging for resources amongst the residue of the earlier years of plenty.

Amongst the survivors, some societies have even been able to preserve intact their civilisation, knowledge and technology, because of their collective genius – that is, the quality of strength, intelligence and self-reliance shared by the whole community. This was manifest, during the onset of glaciation, as an ability to analyse and plan, as a nation, for the long term. Nations of genius, such as France, Germany, the USA, India, Japan, Taiwan, Singapore and Australia, mobilised after 2016 to adapt and evolve, so as to ensure their survival.

France, unique in its high degree of self-sufficiency, escaped the worst effects of the depression, as it had in the 1930s. It successfully deployed its armed forces along its Mediterranean coast to repel wave after wave of refugees from the African continent. Germany also had to fight to seal its long land borders, to unite with Austria and to pacify and absorb the Balkan countries (the former Yugoslavia), to replace land lost to glaciation in the north and to restore access to the sea after the permanent freezing of the Baltic. The United States, turned inwards and subject to military rule, much weakened for several decades after earthquake and tsunami, is now resettling the eastern and western seaboards, and is once again a thriving economy.

Rearranging the deck chairs on the Titanic

During the time of peace and prosperity, Australia, like many other successful western states, became complacent and indolent. The political process was degraded, and the best people worked in industry rather than in the service of the state. Although better-educated than most, the citizenry of Australia had displayed little appetite for collective action since the Second World War, when they rallied round the nation's flag. Earlier, in the decade leading to federation in 1901, the people had displayed great political sophistication through the democratic election of the world's first socialist government in Queensland. During the twentieth century, however, the populace fell into a detached nonchalance, as during the premierships of Howard and Gillard. The corporatisation of journalism, an Australian innovation, had stultified and stifled healthy democratic dialogue.

> The great majority of men and women, in ordinary times, pass through life without ever contemplating or criticising as a whole either their own conditions or those of the world at large.[35]

Australia's industrial capacity had become hollowed out. By the year 2000, Sweden, with less than half the population and one-third of Australia's GDP, had already designed, built and were operating 10 GW of nuclear power generation, supported two local motor vehicle manufacturers, had built its own jet fighters, made its own steel and manufactured its own international brand of electrical appliances. Australia did none of this, because it was easier to dig up and sell minerals to make a quick profit feeding the Asian boom. The state of Victoria, which by 1939 had built and operated 7,600 km of railway track, could no longer adequately maintain the half that remained in use. The simplest of public projects were mismanaged. Australia, which had put 400,000 men into uniform in the First World War, was, by 2010, considering the purchase of cloth for army combat clothing from China. Most of the engineering and construction required for the liquefied natural gas boom of the early years of this century went to foreign contractors because, it was said, Australia did not have the local engineering capacity. Why? Because it had failed to plan, as a nation, to invest in the education and training of the resources required to support its aspirations for development. The only investment criterion was return on capital – an

---

[35] Bertrand Russell, *The Road to Freedom*

accountant's calculation. Too much of the profit from mining and resource extraction went abroad, without adding value locally.

The first alarm

The Crash of 2016 was the critical event which woke the Australian people from the condition of hedonistic apathy into which they had sunk; it compelled the nation, in a way nothing else could have done, to confront the new realities. Demanding times now brought forth remarkable leadership and behaviour.

The Crash left Australia isolated, without trade, sea or air transport. The effect was immediate and brutal. Foreign exchange and interbank lending collapsed in the space of a week. Both the stock market and real estate market also collapsed. The nation soon learnt how dependent it had allowed itself to become on the rest of the world.

After the world's first Great Depression struck in 1929, global trade plunged by more than 50%. Foreign exchange, although distorted by the gold standard, continued. The second time around, almost a century later in 2016, the situation was much worse – trade declined by an estimated 90%. Without the ability to pay for imports and receive payment for exports, all shipping ceased. Ships at sea with cargoes continued to their destination, but were then laid up. Ships across the world, unable to pay to refuel, were stranded in port. Crews deserted and attempted to find their own way home.

For Australia, the heaviest impacts were on fuel supplies, and hence, on transport, and also on unemployment, bank solvency and corporate bankruptcy. Available stocks of gasoline and oil were minimal because, at the eleventh hour, Australia had relied on timely supply from the refineries of south-east Asia; the little fuel available was immediately confiscated by state governments and the armed forces, in order to dedicate it to activities of the highest priority, such as maintaining law and order, the mining of coal, and the supply of food and essential services.

Unlike the Great Depression of the 1930s, when the market for the country's main exports, wool and wheat collapsed, in 2016 farming and agriculture were only mildly affected, and recovered strongly as they converted to feed the domestic market. After 2016, the previously dominant exporting industries – minerals, coal, gas and aluminium – failed, when the foreign exchange system, which had become a corporate casino, collapsed totally. In the 1930s, when a rudimentary exchange system endured, trade had not fallen much more than 50%.

In 1938, unemployment in Australia had peaked at 23% in a workforce still feeling the losses of the First World War; after 2016 it peaked at 45%. The burden of unemployment fell most heavily on metropolitan areas and corporate communities. Much of the manufacturing industry ceased production because no one was spending to buy its products and export was impossible without foreign exchange. Without fuel, many employees were unable to travel to work. Essential businesses were able to struggle on by providing pooled transport for workers. Construction halted while new capital investments were postponed and layoffs were widespread, most especially in export industries. A few enlightened businesses, with a vision for the future, retained their people, albeit often at reduced pay, and began the difficult process of adjustment.

For the first time in Australia's history, a national state of emergency was declared. Parliaments were suspended, and the armed forces and police were mobilised and given extraordinary powers. Public services were preserved; the essential services of electricity, water supply, sewage and waste removal managed to cope, supported by the confiscation of fuel supplies. Australia was fortunate indeed to be able to preserve the national information and telecommunications systems, which enabled remarkable efforts of coordination and allowed some employees to work from home.

Agriculture, for long the poor, country relation and neglected while investment was channelled to the large cities, now became the focus of intense interest. The farms were capable of producing many crops for export markets that were now closed; the challenge was not only to provide sufficient food, but to produce fuel for cultivation and transport. No one starved; the staples were always available, although, at first, when distribution failed, many went hungry.

Damage control

In the initial chaos, banks in Australia closed their doors. Many businesses and individuals found themselves without money. A system of local barter rapidly arose, based on the supply and exchange of food, water, energy and labour. Everywhere, IOUs were signed between individuals against the day when currency stability would return. This widespread local exchange became so useful that it gradually evolved into a system of local currency and co-operative banking. Interestingly, such a system had evolved after the sovereign default of Argentina, where, by 2003, twenty provinces had issued their own currencies. Thus, now, in 2053, in Australia, seventeen of twenty counties in the southern state of Victoria still have their own banks and their own currencies. The economy has been decentralised. People tend to obtain most of their requirements locally, with little need for the common currency operated by the federal government.

Australia got back to business quicker than most. Industry and business saw the clear need to turn inwards, to make the country self-sufficient and immune from future shocks. In practise, that meant rebuilding domestic production capacity for everything from steel to clothing, from ships to renewable electricity generation. Agriculture was the first to recover; country people had always been the most self-sufficient and independent. Crop prices increased initially owing to shortages in some staples. In the space of a year, wheat crops gave way to rape and Siberian Oilseed (*Camelina Sativa*), to be crushed for oil. Biodiesel was produced by mixing the oil with ethanol and caustic soda, a process so simple that many farmers at first made their own fuel, until small co-operatives sprang up in rural towns to produce a more standardised product. Within two years, all diesel-driven vehicles and equipment in Australia were back in use, a feat only bettered in France. Biodiesel, which has a similar gross calorific value to jet fuel and aviation gasoline, was substituted for Jet-A, allowing aircraft to return to the skies.

Excess wheat was converted to ethanol, at first in makeshift fermentation and distillation plants that appeared at every rural grain silo; more sophisticated designs rapidly evolved. Conversion of petrol engines to ethanol use was a simple job, and so Australia found itself on the road again.

Electricity supply was the second variable in the energy equation. In the year before the Crash of 2016, Australia had consumed 235 billion kWh of energy. Of this, 80% was generated by burning coal, making the intensity of greenhouse gas emissions the highest of any OECD country. Widespread shutdown of industry, in particular aluminium smelting, cut consumption in half. As with food, the only challenge to maintaining supply was the ability to fuel mining machinery and to transport the coal to generators. In the short term, nothing was to stop the country from burning coal, which regrettably continued to feed climate change. Energy policy had always been controversial in Australia and the government had always taken the easy way out. In the longer term, as international trade was restored, Australia faced the prospect of global ostracism unless it acted to reduce carbon dioxide production.

Banks were nationalised and opened their doors again but found their retail operations, for long their bread and butter, replaced by local upstarts. The Australian federal government printed money freely to pay government employees, and issued food vouchers to the unemployed. The manufacturing workforce slowly returned to work, beginning the arduous process of retooling to produce the goods that had previously been imported and the things people now needed. By 2025 the car industry was fully converted to the manufacture of agricultural and construction equipment, buses, new trains, power generators, and modular diesel and ethanol processing equipment to replace the first makeshift installations.

Clawing back international trade after the Crash of 2016 was a painful process for Australia. With their Chinese markets gone, some industries never recovered. Investors in aluminium production had to concede that their assets were useless, stranded and of no future value. Production of iron ore gradually resumed, but export quantities never again approached more than 15% of installed capacity. Trade in uranium flourished, the one commodity that the rest of the world desired above all else. In the decade after 2016, international exchange did not exist, and traders reverted to barter on a cargo-by-cargo basis. Universal distrust of trading currencies in use before the Crash, such as the dollar or yen, led to the adoption of gold as the currency of foreign exchange. Individual states were then able to effectively establish their own exchange rate by reference to gold.

The sinking ship

In the midst of this frantic reorientation of the whole Australian society and economy, a realisation grew in the national psyche that this unprecedented depression was but a precursor to an even more fundamental crisis lying ahead: sudden and unpredictable climate change. All the signs were of impending catastrophe, but very few Australians had any idea how they should plan and prepare for eventualities they could not predict. Despite a reasonable understanding of how the Earth functioned, the people could not guess when change would affect them, or what the outcome might be; the global cooling scenario was plausible, but the idea of a hotter climate had been around for longer. What was the planning scenario? What could be done to be prepared?

For many years, some farsighted Australians had been advocating effective action against climate change, but the ideas and concepts, although discussed and understood, had never caught fire. The shocking aftermath of the Crash in 2016 provided the spark that set alight all the intellectual fuel which had accumulated.

At first, those most active in the debate were young people, who saw that they were the ones who were destined to lead us through these years. Unemployment had fallen most heavily on the highly educated young, who responded with protest and aggressive agitation in pursuit of their views. For the first time, Australia faced a truly widespread student movement. At the other end of the demographic scale were older people, mostly retired, who had seen their pensions destroyed and their dreams of a comfortable end to their lives shattered. These two groups, combining their wisdom and energy, began the national conversation.

Thus, a political debate grew up of a quality and pervasiveness never experienced before in Australia, based on a profound critique of capitalism and growth, and intensely focused on national security and survival. Much of the early discussion was of 'lifeboat ethics', the morality of the single-minded pursuit of one's own safety. By late in 2018, the debate had engulfed the whole of the nation; all the political parties were engaged and, for perhaps the first time, they found common ground for agreement.

At last Australians understood that the Earth was not created for the sole benefit of its present inhabitants, and just as the human species was threatened, so were many others. People realized that they did not have a right to crowd out other species and forms of life. Because of the power humans wield, it was seen as a moral duty to protect other species as well, and to leave things in the world just the way they had been found. Gradually a new vision and strategy for Australia's place in the world emerged.[36] Key elements of that strategy were:

- renewable resources should be harvested at rates that do not exceed regeneration rates
- the rate of depletion of non-renewable resources should not exceed the rate of creation of renewable substitutes
- waste emission rates should not exceed the natural assimilative capacities of ecosystems into which they are emitted.

This was a new concept for Australia, where national planning had never progressed much beyond each party's manifesto for the next three years. Realising that climate change was inevitable, the view formed of this island continent as a 'lifeboat' in which could be preserved a significant population of people with all the knowledge, the civilisation and the standards of development that the years of plenty had delivered. This vision touched on the way Australia would manage economically, the way it would govern itself, and how it would involve itself in world affairs. There was a determination that the nation must be able to go it alone, never again allowing itself to become dependent on the outside world. These were long-held values in the national psyche, despite them having fallen temporarily into disuse.

---

[36] H. E. Daly, *Toward Some Operational Principles of Sustainable Development*

Preparing the lifeboat

Public debate led to a statement of principles which were to guide the future direction of the Australian nation:

- The nation must prepare itself for the coming climate transition.
- The carrying capacity of the land must be understood and not exceeded.
- Australia must remain self-sufficient, self-reliant, unaligned and independent, but continue to communicate and to trade with the world.
- The carbon dioxide dumped into the Earth's atmosphere since 1800 has not been assimilated, but has rather induced global heating, and should be reversed at the earliest opportunity.
- Australia will make no further net discharge of carbon dioxide to the atmosphere from non-renewable resources.
- Water taken from the environment for human use will be returned to the environment in the same or better condition.
- All non-renewable resources consumed will be replaced by renewable substitutes. The harvesting of forests will be balanced by the planting of new forests containing an equivalent composition of species. No further forest clearance will be permitted and agricultural land will be husbanded to preserve fertility.
- All use of hydrocarbons for energy production (oil, gas and coal) will be replaced by safe and sustainable biological, nuclear or solar processes.
- These goals can only be achieved without growth.

This nation-wide resolve engendered a new sense of purpose and alignment. Bipartisan agreement between the two main political parties empowered the people chosen to lead and steady the nation through the dark times to come. Work began on a national strategy and plan.

The new framework would have to embody the localisation, or decentralisation of communities, which had occurred spontaneously. The people had to be equipped to respond flexibly to this more democratic and participative way of organising a society. In practice this meant an urgent programme of education and training to prepare people for the likely challenges. To underpin this, the sum total of knowledge of all mankind had to be gathered together, while it was still accessible, and preserved for the future.

Out of these policies came a national plan, the *Lifeboat Australia* strategy. In 2019, its first year, the strategy was long on vision, but short on specific action. This was the first ever national plan, unlike countries like France[37] which had prepared five-year plans since 1958. Bit by bit, the plan evolved to encompass the big issues:

- The people, their well-being and purpose – individual, family community and national life
- The constitution – how it was to be organised in order for the people to govern themselves
- Educating and training people to assure national self-reliance
- Future energy needs and how they would be met
- The retention of human knowledge and technology
- Management of population at a sustainable level
- Business, banking and their role in Australia's economy
- The defence and security of the nation
- Law and order
- Town planning
- Taxation and compensation
- International trade

In 2020, the national constitutional convention met in the national capital, Canberra, to revise the constitution and bring into law the many changes needed to support the way the country was to be governed in the future. The fact that it was held at all was a

---

[37] www.emprunt-national-2010.fr

measure of the huge groundswell of support that the proposals enjoyed across the land; this was the most sweeping revision since it first went into force with the federation of the Australian states in 1901. This time, in 2020, the driving force was not for centralism, but for decentralisation, to embody in law the devolution of powers from federal and state governments to county and parish.

The other significant addition was the Declaration of Rights, favoured by some delegates to the convention of 1898 but not approved. The agreed declaration, as in 1898, was derived from the US Declaration of Rights, but successfully addressed the right of well-being and the individual's right to an equal share of the national resource asset base; to balance these rights, it added Obligations, among them limits on individual income, and duties to preserve the environment and to limit the nation's population.

With great sadness, the constitutional monarchy in the United Kingdom, for period a central part of Australia's political make-up, was abandoned and a new republic established. The head of state, Charles III, who had become known as the Green King for his wise and tireless advocacy of the environment, had been an important influence through his lifelong campaign for sustainable ways of living. Sadly, his remoteness in distant London was no longer practical. After a long gestation, the Australian republic was at last born.

Launching the lifeboat

An almost immediate decision was made to end immigration and population growth. A consensus of understanding had rapidly evolved that zero economic growth had to happen at some time, that it may as well happen immediately, and that a steady-state economy was only possible with zero population growth. In ancient times, the aborigines had survived only through rigorous control of population. The hardening resolve apparent in Australia in these difficult decades recognised that, to avoid the lifeboat being swamped and sunk with the loss of all lives, there had to be a limit to the number of occupants. Others across the world had already recognised this, such as Lee Kuan Yew, who once said of boat people seeking refuge in Singapore:

> If you don't have calluses on your heart you will bleed to death.[38]

National borders were closed to all except returning citizens, who had been straggling their way back as international transport slowly resumed. All non-resident aliens were repatriated as soon as transport became available.

The consumption of resources was brought under control; over the ten years to 2030, stringent environmental controls were gradually imposed at both ends of the value chain. During this period, oil, gas and coal production were permitted, but only under licence to organisations committed to installing nuclear, wind, wave or geothermal energy supply, on condition that they return the energy sold as free electricity supplied by their new generating capacity. The adoption of renewable fuels for vehicles, ships and aircraft had already been forced by the cessation of imports in 2016.

Thus in the decade 2020 to 2030, carbon dioxide discharge was cut by 10% per year. Waste water quality was improved step by step until it met natural standards; this was a great imposition on the economic viability of Australian cities, which had previously dumped raw or partially treated sewage directly into the oceans; it led to a continuing decentralisation of people from cities to rural communities. The effect of laws restraining resource consumption

---

[38] Lee Kuan Yew, of the boat people attempting to land on Singapore, Nov 78

was to encourage the maintenance of the existing stock of assets rather than write off their value and build anew.

Interestingly, some countries had already adopted zero or negative growth spontaneously and involuntarily, such as Japan between 1990 and 2016. The years leading up to 2016 had seen many frantic, duplicitous struggles to resume growth while reducing consumption and discharges. Eventually, a fatalistic acceptance of the inevitability of 'stagnation' led to a confrontation of how best to make it advantageous. Although there was a general desire to limit growth, it was thought that this action should not impede development, which, it was hoped, would continue to improve the quality of life and well-being in Australia.

During this time, unemployment across the world reached tragic proportions, leading to severe poverty, not just in the third world, but in many nations of the first world as well. Laws were passed to limit work times, provide top-up education and training, and lower the social security net. Corporation law was amended to ensure a closer relationship between firms and the communities in which they lived; European countries such as France, Norway and Germany had already been successful in this regard. New legislation limited individual earnings of the richest to no more than ten times the minimum wage. Some thought this would impair development by removing incentives for the best minds, but what was found in Australia was that the best minds were willing to work for values other than money. Corporate life has undoubtedly now become less aggressive and more benign.

'Investment' in Australia became a far more complex concept. The first few years after the Crash saw a moratorium on bank lending for commercial investment. Successive governments filled the gap with extensive spending on public works so as to sustain economic activity and get Australia back on its feet.

Much of this work pertained to the dispersal of the inhabitants of the coastal cities. In time, this was followed by an upsurge of investment by successful small and medium enterprises, funded from their own revenue.

Rather than increasing production by increasing throughput of resources, there was a move to fix or reduce resource throughput and encourage improvements in productivity that reduced resource use per unit of output. In so doing, Australia has been able to economise on materials and energy taken from the environment. The lesson learnt has been to work smarter, not harder. Through concentration on good design and planning, the nation is now able to manufacture its own ships, aircraft, electronics, weapons systems and nuclear power plants; the intensity of the technology is now as great as if the country were on a war footing, which perhaps it is. As a result, continuing improvement in quality of life is visible: people enjoy increased leisure, better health and medical care, and are able to devote, each year, slightly more resources to pure research, education and the arts.

Reaching safe harbour

International trade gradually rebounded, but with the worldwide, devastating reduction in population, to only a fraction of the volume once experienced. International trade had always been a mixed blessing. Before 2016, every nation aspired to export-led growth; however, globally, all exports and imports had to sum to zero. So it was impossible for any one country to run a trade surplus without at least one other running a deficit. The result was that many countries paid for trade with a loss of autonomy, reduced self-sufficiency, and high unemployment among low-skilled, low-income employees, while other nations paid with increasing debt and interest burden. And there is no doubt that transporting huge quantities of raw materials overseas, as

Australia had once done, had caused untold environmental damage.

Consumption of goods inevitably fell, but the loss was cosmetic. Australians are now happily doing without things they never needed in the first place: Gucci handbags, carbonated, sweetened water in aluminium containers, all-terrain vehicles to drive the children to school, vacations in Bali – the list is staggering. This was helped by the strict control of advertising, which now provides only factual information, rather than attempting to seduce Australian consumers with false promises of happiness and better lives.

And so it was that nature intervened in the human condition and compelled the Earth's inhabitants to become serious about survival and change their ways. For someone like me who grew up in rural Victoria in the south- east of Australia, the renaissance of rural communities, after fifty years of drift to the coastal cities, made huge sense; it had always seemed to me that dispersal of population, rather than concentration, offered a higher quality of well-being with a lighter ecological footprint.

Australia had the good fortune to be able to respond quickly enough to avert complete disaster; other nations of genius also prepared for impending climate change, but survival was predominately a function of the luck of geography. Some states remained immersed in self-absorption, incompetence and disorganisation, and their societies, unable to make the transition, went into decline. Fortunately, enough of mankind survived, I think, to assure the endurance of our species. But can we say for sure that civilisation will endure, or that those who survive now in primitive chaos will not one day evolve to challenge and compete with us? In the final two chapters we will consider the state of Australian society and national institutions and their fitness for the eternal struggle to endure.

FIVE

This fortress

This other Eden, demi-paradise,
This fortress built by Nature for herself
Against infection and the hand of war,
This happy breed of men, this little world,
This precious stone set in the silver sea,
Which serves it in the office of a wall
Or as a moat defensive to a house
Against the envy of less happier lands ...[39]

These words, written at another time in history and relating to another place, are nevertheless as appropriate to the Australia of today as they were to the Britain of Richard II. The nation now resembles a vast castle protected by surrounding seas.

The failure of 'big government'

In the early twentieth century, the governments of the wealthiest states, including Australia, had become progressively more ineffective. They had grown into large inefficient bureaucracies that sapped the people's wealth to fund grandiose schemes such as the European Union, the ill-conceived organisation that brought Europe to its economic knees in 2014. In Australia, the federal government had progressively extended its powers. The role of the Federal Commonwealth was never envisaged, by the founding fathers, to be much more than a currency union enabling free trade between the states, and the sharing of a common

---

[39] William Shakespeare, *Richard II*

responsibility for defence; federation was a modest, enlightened undertaking. Andrew Fisher, early Australian Labour prime minister (during the period 1908 - 1915) and formerly a working man, walked to his office in Spring Street from his private residence in a suburban street in St Kilda in Melbourne.

There is a misconception that large states exist to foster a common culture, language, customs and the welfare of the people. An alternative view is that, in fact, they have arisen to allow political and economic elites – oligopolies – to expand their businesses, garner overseas colonies and establish more expansive trading markets. In time, the federal government in Australia grew into a parasitical octopus, with tentacles touching every aspect of the people's lives. In doing so, it took over the taxation rights of the states, which permanently curtailed their effectiveness. Karl Marx foresaw this result when he wrote on capitalist society:

> It has drowned the most heavenly ecstasies of religious fervour, of chivalrous enthusiasm, of philistine sentimentalism, in the icy water of egotistical calculation. It has resolved personal worth into exchange value, and in the place of the numberless indefeasible chartered freedoms, has set up that single, unconscionable freedom – free trade.[40]

When the Federal Constitutional Convention of 2020 opened in Canberra under the spectre of impending climate change, it was unanimously agreed that the gravest challenges facing humanity were population management, energy supply and adaptation to climate change, all challenges which big government had failed to tackle. Out-of-control population growth, profligate energy consumption and the production of excessive green-house gas, were seen as the drivers of climate change. At that time, the populace still hoped for a soft landing and actively sought this in global forums, where legal and social systems to constrain and

---

[40] Carl Marx, *Das Capital*

reduce population, and an urgent strategy of research and development of nuclear and renewable energy were advocated. In the face of such wide-reaching goals, the convention enabled the Lifeboat Australia programme, even though many thought, or perhaps hoped, that it was an unnecessary contingency plan.

Devolved government

An objective of the Convention of 2020 was to legitimise the flow of power back to local and state governments from the national government. Australia had turned inwards, so there was little need at first for foreign affairs or trade or commerce. The main activities of the federal government became defence, telecommunications and the management of the national currency. The primary concerns of the people were food, water supply, housing and security, and for this they had taken matters into their own hands or formed ad hoc community-action groups. These had coalesced into county-like organisations based on the old shires and cities, with elected councils, leaders and police superintendents, in effect adopting many aspects of the US county and French commune systems.

The outcome of the Convention was to allow diversity by restoring the influence of local communities over government, to 'let one hundred flowers bloom', so that never again would centrally directed development harm the commons. City and shire councils demanded and got a greater say in the management of all aspects of community life. Public demand mobilised behind a proposed amendment to formalise the subdivision of each state into counties, which would, in addition to their existing local government powers, assume authority for education, hospitals, police, criminal law, company registration and banking. The state of Victoria, for example, was subdivided into thirty-seven counties. The role of the federal government was curtailed, along the lines of the Swiss federal government system, akin to that of a night watchman in a city. To avoid the central state from being all-powerful ever again, and to assure that it remained the steward of the collective interests of the people, counties and states, the right to assess taxes was transferred to the counties.

Australia's first constitution in 1901 was substantially modelled on that of the United States, and although the USA had for many years suffered from a decline in standards of public life, the convention of 2020 adopted additional aspects, such as the election of county sheriffs, to take policing closer to the community. The breakup of the banking industry under the Glass-Steagall Act after the Wall Street Crash of 1929, was evaluated as model for converting the Australian banking industry from an unguided missile of corporate greed to a community service. As a result, retail banking and lending was constrained to operate on a county by county basis, while control over commercial banking reverted to each state.

Local co-operatives – a new business model

In the years leading to the Crash, commercial companies had grown too large. Mergers and acquisitions had created huge, unwieldy, insensitive behemoths that destroyed more value than they created. They had grown to such a size that they lost touch with their stakeholders, the people they existed to benefit, and instead became subject to the ego of their chief executives and their bands of ruthless acolytes. Firms such as Shell and BP became truly dangerous, with strings of fatal accidents and environmental disasters. Tax avoidance was rife, and firms felt no sense of obligation or gratitude to the communities that had granted them their mandates to exist. Employment terms were weakened; people were treated as production units, employed or dismissed according to short term priorities.

When the Australian stock exchange crashed following the foreign exchange collapse in 2016, some ninety per cent of listed firms were unable to attract buyers for their stock, rendering them worthless. Many of these organisations had already been shut down by the freeze on bank commercial lending and the cessation of international trade, and were de facto bankrupt. Their physical assets remained, but they were worthless to creditors because no one wanted to buy them. There was no point in creditors taking over organisations which had nothing but liabilities and worthless assets. In an attempt to wipe the slate clean, state governments took ownership of physical assets in return for allowing a total write-off of financial liabilities owed to or by corporations.

Something quite remarkable occurred in the months after the crash of 2016 – the multinational corporations were consigned to the dustbin of history. As rural communities got to grips with food supply and fuel production, community and employee-owned co-operatives began to form spontaneously. These organisations harked back a century to the early agricultural co-operatives and, led by men and women dedicated to their communities rather than ripping out personal gain, they thrived. Observing how successful the model was, state governments began to invite proposals for takeovers and the operation of sequestered physical assets. Often it was groups of former employees who stepped forward with operating proposals and, when a proposal was accepted, an equal share of ownership was transferred to each and every employee. The shareholders would then elect a board of directors, who from their number would elect a chairman. Chief executives were appointed by the chairman but could be challenged and vetoed by the elected board. It was a remarkable process, more orderly than the carve-up of assets by the oligarchs of Russia after the demise of communism, yet more informal than the privatisation of East German industry in the same period.

Commerce

Companies that were behaving as if they were immune to the laws of the market – that is, who considered themselves too big to fail – contributed much of the impetus of the crash of 2016. While small and medium-sized businesses competed for survival, the global corporations were seemingly immune. Not only did they distort competition, they subverted the 'survival of the fittest' ethos which lay at the heart of capitalism by running to government in tears whenever things got tough. The new challenge was to find a way in which the benefits of market-driven efficiency could be retained, while assuring that the rights of taxpayers, employees and consumers were preserved. This was uncannily reminiscent of the period in the history of the USA around 1911, when government rethought how big business worked by dismantling the so-called 'trusts':

> We have here the problem of bigness.... The Curse of Bigness shows how size can become a menace--both industrial and social. It can be an industrial menace because it creates gross inequalities against existing or putative competitors. It can be a social menace.... In final analysis, size in steel is the measure of the power of a handful of men over our economy.... The philosophy of the Sherman Act is that it should not exist.... Industrial power should be decentralized. It should be scattered into many hands so that the fortunes of the people will not be dependent on the whim or caprice, the political prejudices, the emotional stability of a few self-appointed men.... That is the philosophy and the command of the Sherman Act. It is founded on a theory of hostility to the concentration in private hands of power so great that only a government of the people should have it.[41]

---

[41] Dissenting opinion of Justice Douglas in *United States* v. *Columbia Steel Co.*

This was the era when the Standard Oil trust was broken up into 30 different companies and the banking industry dismantled. Community banking was introduced, with banks allowed to open branches only in their state of residence, and later, being required to split their commercial and investment businesses. Small *was* beautiful for a while, until the lessons of history were forgotten and bigness returned to vogue.

Circumstances in Australia after the crash of 2016 conspired to create a new model of industry and commerce in which ownership and assets were dispersed rather than centralised. When I say new, however, it was little different to how things were in the late twentieth century in Germany and northern Italy, where small and medium enterprises, often privately or family-owned, provided an astonishing range of high-tech materials, equipment and services.

This model of industry has largely continued to the present day when, in 2053, businesses in Australia which continue to be governed by state law, must now be registered in a county, and may only employ and conduct their primary business within that county. So, we find some counties mainly occupied with a single major business, for instance, agriculture, running a mine or manufacturing power modules, while others are home to many smaller businesses and services. The whole complex system of interrelationship is made possible only by Australia's ability to sustain a national information and telecommunication system. In thus taking the work to the people, rather than the people to the work, this country has undone one of the most negative innovations of the Industrial Revolution.

Money

The majority of Australian banks failed in the crash of 2016. The cash left in circulation was not nearly enough to allow employers to pay workers and for everyone to purchase the necessities of life, so employers issued IOUs, which were accepted by local businesses, to be interchangeable for hard currency when it became available again.

With the few remaining banks reluctant to lend money, people began to arrange loans personally. This informal system depended on trust more than on law, but had the benefit that the borrowing was local and the lenders had a good idea of how secure were the loans that they were making. Soon, deposit-taking organisations opened in many communities to widen the scope of lending, and these eventually coalesced into the county banks we see today.

In the many post-mortems of the crash, it became abundantly clear that one of the worst aspects of the old system was 'fractional reserve banking', whereby banks could lend money they did not have on the assumption that not all depositors would demand their money back at the same time. It was a kind of Ponzi scheme in which money was created out of nothing.

The Constitutional Convention in 2020 resolved that, in future, banks, as they were re-established, must operate with full reserve. In practice, this meant that only two kinds of account would be available: custodial, where money deposited would be available anytime; and investment, where money invested for a fixed time could be loaned by the bank, but only for a similar term. So, if every single customer wanted to withdraw their money at the same time, the bank would be able to repay them. Banks were permitted to charge a fee for looking after depositors' money in custodial accounts. Investment accounts would pay a one-off fee to term investors, but charge borrowers an arrangement fee. Interest was abolished, along with fractional reserve banking. Borrowers would now compete for loans by offering the bank a nominated share of the profit from their investment, and the bank would loan money to those borrowers offering the best return and those considered most likely to deliver their promise. Each year, the bank would pay a share of profit to its investment depositors, based on the success of their loan portfolio. Banks and depositors would share the risks and the rewards of borrowers' investments, unused money would be invested to best effect and the highest value investment opportunities would be pursued.

Now, in 2053, the results are clear to see. Banks and businesses exist for the betterment of their employees and owners, who are often the same people. They belong to a community and behave like community members. Waste products cannot be discharged outside the county, unless by commercial agreement with the county of disposal. Users may, if they wish, return equipment and materials at the end of their life to the county from which they originated, for disposal or reuse. Pollution is avoided because disposal can occur only locally, and disposal costs are included in any purchase price. People no longer commute to work by car; they walk or cycle. Australia, having achieved decentralisation and localism on a grand scale, has managed to reverse the once inexorable trend to wholesale urbanism.

Energy and life

It seems to me that a good indicator of the state of development or well-being of a society is the availability of energy to perform work. Primitive man did everything himself, and the ratio of input of human energy to the amount of energy output was one to one. One person could lift, carry or work; two people could do twice as much, and so on. Think of medieval treadmills and tableaux of ancient Egyptian statues being pulled by hundreds of people. Early man harnessed the horse to plough, carry, lift and pull, and the energy required to grow, feed and lead the horse was a fraction of the energy that the horse produced. Wind was harnessed with great skill to push ships and drive mills, and the energy required to build and operate the ships was a fraction of the energy harvested from the wind. Waterpower was utilised to drive mills and forges. Canal transport amplified the effectiveness of horsepower by reducing the amount of work lost through friction. Other animals were also tamed and used for work, and it is interesting to remember how many species were tamed and the diversity of uses to which they were put, and what a short time ago that was. This is the nature of an essential model for effective and efficient living – symbiosis.

A great breakthrough, which freed us from man and animal power, was the invention of the steam engine in 1698. First developed for dewatering the mines of England, it was soon put to use pumping clean water into cities and taking away the sewage. With no means of transporting steam power over great distances, big clumsy steam engines had to be at the heart of a city, factory or mine, encouraging the trend towards centralisation which began with the Industrial Revolution. Steam power was adapted for ships, which led to more efficient sea transport and an increase in global trade. By freeing mankind from the menial tasks of fetching and carrying, it allowed us to devote more and more of our energy to improving the human condition. And so we progressed, with the invention of electric power, the use of hydrocarbon fuels, and the harnessing of nuclear power. Each step freed us from more drudgery, enabling ever more creativity and reflection. Or did it?

The leveraging of human capability and the appetite for ever greater amounts of energy rapidly overwhelmed the natural resources of the planet. Just as the early Industrial Revolution in England had quickly consumed the ancient oak forests to provide charcoal for energy, so world consumption of oil, and excessive carbon dioxide discharge soon reached their limits. And, as the risks of energy production – coal seam gas and nuclear, to name two – grew ever more potent, the consequences of carelessness worsened. This was always the predominant objection to nuclear power -- that incompetence, greed and political avarice lead inevitably to projects that are unsafe and harmful. As the twentieth-first century progressed, the truth of this warning became horribly apparent.

The production of energy in Australia

This was the energy scene when the economic crash overtook the world in 2016. Australia had depended largely on coal, along with gas and some hydropower; even brown coal was burnt, which was appallingly polluting. Coal reserves were plentiful but gas was running out; rapacious foreign investors were too readily allowed to export the remaining reserves of natural gas. The contribution of hydropower was dropping as the climate became drier. A significant proportion of electricity was used to manufacture aluminium, a metal so plentiful that the world had to invent for it new and scarcely necessary uses, such as making containers for soft drinks.

Railway electrification was minimal and road transport vehicles were fuelled by petrol and oil. Domestic production and refining capacity had declined because it had been cheaper to import refined products from south-east asia. Fuel was imported on a 'just in time basis', to avoid tying money up in stock, and so emergency supplies were negligible.

Earlier in this book, I reflected on the immediate impact of the Crash on fuel supplies, the rapid remobilisation of agricultural production and the conversion of air and road transport to biofuels. As luck would have it, internal combustion and turbine engines are readily converted to biofuels: biodiesel is of a comparable CV (calorific value) to mineral diesel oil, while the CV of ethanol is two-thirds that of gasoline. And so, to this day, the old trucks, trains, ships and airplanes rumble on. They are replaced only when they can no longer be repaired. There is no need for replacing cars with new models every three years; they are simply a means of transport and no longer a symbol of manliness or a badge of achievement.

In the years after the Crash, the whole world was panicked into reducing carbon dioxide emissions, too late as things turned out, but an absolutely necessary precondition for mankind's long-term survival. A strong global treaty was rapidly drafted and signed in haste in 2017, committing signatories to crash programmes of green-house gas abatement; those who declined to sign, or who no longer possessed competent national governments, were ostracised and isolated.

The Australian response was to adopt nuclear power as a replacement for coal, but with stringent safeguards. It took time, but now, in 2053, Australia relies entirely on wind, hydro and nuclear for the generation of its electricity.

Back when the climate was drying, hydropower could not be relied on. After the onset of glaciation in 2031 the Australian climate moderated and rainfall across the country increased. As a result, more water has become available for hydroelectricity, which is entirely complementary with intermittent wind power and base-load nuclear generation; hydro is now used during peak periods, because it can be started and stopped easily, and nuclear for base-load demand, since it cannot be turned up or down so readily.

I should mention the minor role wood played in Australia as a short-term energy source. Aboriginal society understood the importance of keeping forests clear of dead wood and flammable material, to assure much cooler and less-damaging bush fires. In the first years after the Crash, crews of unemployed people across the country were given the task of removing the enormous quantities of dead wood in the undergrowth of forests; this wood was used for domestic and industrial heat, although some valuable timber was also obtained. At the same time, areas of abandoned or untilled land, particularly in the coastal regions, were replanted with a mix of native species, to increase coastal rainfall and reverse desertification. The extraction of wood for fuel continues to this day, but at a much reduced, and sustainable level.

Following the Crash, neither natural gas nor coal could be exported. The nation continued to rely on coal for electricity generation until the flow of gas could be redirected from the redundant gas fields of Queensland and Western Australia towards the electricity generators in the south and east. Breathing space was needed for a nuclear industry to be built from scratch.

Modular nuclear power

Prior to the Crash of 2016, Australia had not shown the slightest interest in nuclear power; there were no research institutes to speak of, the education of nuclear physicists and engineers was negligible, and suitable equipment, materials and construction capacity were non-existent. The windfall profits earned from the export of our minerals, gas and coal had been squandered on the further development of mining and gas production assets, which lay abandoned on the north-west coast and in Queensland.

The Crash provoked immediate action. It was obvious that the nation did not have, nor would it ever have, the resources to research and develop indigenous reaction processes. A pragmatic evaluation, worldwide, of the processes available selected for development two fast neutron reactor processes with obvious benefits: PRISM, developed by GE-Hitachi, and the TWR (Travelling Wave Reactor) developed by Terrapower.

These processes provide high fuel efficiency because they release the full potential energy of the uranium fuel, instead of around one percent as in the earlier conventional power reactors. Thus refuelling intervals are long, as much as twenty years. They operate at atmospheric pressure, using a liquid-metal heat transfer fluid, either sodium, lead or lead-bismuth, to transfer heat from the nuclear reactor to the steam generator, making containment safer than with a pressurised system. Most importantly, the actual fission reactions are inherently safe; in a fast neutron process, an increase in core temperature slows the reaction rather than accelerates it. The circulation of heat transfer fluid is driven by convection, eliminating the complication and hazard of pumps to circulate the transfer fluid; in the event of emergency shutdown, natural convection is also sufficient to cool an overheated core. After start-up with processed fuel, the fast neutron process breeds its own fuel, a necessity because Australia has no domestic capacity for uranium processing.

The PRISM process concept was designed initially for the US Department of Energy, but inexplicably cancelled in 1994, just as construction of a pilot plant was to begin. It was originally conceived to be fuelled by the waste from conventional heavy water reactors and to generate 622 MWe of power. In Australia it was modified and simplified to a 100MWe unit.

The TWR process is designed to burn slowly through a block of fuel, of either depleted or natural uranium; it requires a small amount of enriched uranium to start the reaction, which then breeds and consumes the actual fuel as it burns through the block. Elsewhere in the world, plants based on this process burn depleted fuel, which has been stored as a waste product of less-efficient heavy water processes. Australia chose to use unprocessed uranium as the raw material, of which the country still possesses ninety per cent of known world reserves. Possession of these reserves gave Australia the leverage to barter with France for the supply of enough enriched fuel to initiate the first wave of installations. Refuelling and reprocessing onsite is avoided simply by sealing the process, rather like a battery, and returning reactor modules to the factory for refuelling after long periods in operation. The inherent simplicity of the design makes it relatively easy to build and even easier to operate.

Australia's changeover to renewable forms of energy generation over the last thirty years has led to a dispersal of power-generation capacity. Before the Crash of 2016, the conventional wisdom had been to construct large, centralised generation plants; this choice was driven partly by the type and location of fuel, but largely by perceived economic benefits of scale. As society localised, there was as upsurge in the number of small generation units, and a kind of energy internet developed, in which power suppliers were dispersed, just like consumers. The electric power companies which were established in every county wanted independence of supply, and much smaller 'packaged' designs quickly evolved to meet their needs.

The fast neutron processes were ideal for modularisation[42,43] into smaller units. A concept evolved of standard generation plants of 100 MWe – 'designed once, built often' – which could be manufactured in modular form and transported to site by road or rail. It has now become evident that, with smaller units, there is far more opportunity to apply the lessons learned in operation to the design of evermore efficient and safe plant. Quality of

---

[42] www.theoildrum.com, Possibilities for Small Modular Nuclear Reactors? 20 Jul 10
[43] World Nuclear Association, Small Nuclear Power Reactors, 30 Sep 11

manufacture of a standard design under factory conditions is much superior to that achieved in one-off, on-site, construction, so that safety is greatly enhanced.

Fortunately after the Crash there were a large number of defunct automobile factories which could be readily converted to manufacture of power units. Design and fabrication skills existed in Australia for the manufacture of materials, equipment, parts, and assembly; all that was needed was to draw them together.

Reflections

To a great extent, the reformation of the Australian way of governance was simply the adoption of customs that events had brought forth. Earlier democratic arrangements, including the European Economic Community, the United Nations, and even federations of states, such as the USA, had failed in their stewardship of the human race. The humbling reality was that these outmoded political processes were incapable of governing a world population, and that despite its humanist ideals, mankind could conceive of no other way of shaping the future than to watch helplessly as famine, pestilence, war and disaster had their remorseless way. In other words, mankind was driven forward into the future more by chance than by conscious intention.

And so, under the stress of unavoidable, irreversible change, Australia managed to evolve a system of value and exchange that replaced the use of monetary growth. Now, in 2053, where ever organised society still exists in the world, the experience has been remarkably similar. In other places, where chaos reigns, there has been a reversion to barter and even worse, cargo cults; some still rely on fossil fuels, although the overall world production of greenhouse gas is now low. How these societies will evolve is anybody's guess, and for those who live to see it and survive, it will be an interesting story.

Even more interesting will be what becomes of energy growth. Australia has adopted fast-breeder technology, and with it potential access to virtually unlimited fuel supplies, thanks to the large quantities of uranium fuel, stored as waste in repositories across the world, or as ore remaining in the ground. Amazingly, for the first time in history, this nation has possible access to an unlimited source of energy that will not produce greenhouse gases, nor add to the risk of irreversibly damaging the atmosphere with poisonous isotopes. As a nation, it has not even begun to explore the opportunities this could offer. How will energy use grow, what unimaginable benefits will be derived from it? And how will Australian society thus evolve?

SIX

A brave new world

O, wonder! How many goodly creatures are there here!

How beauteous mankind is! O brave new world!

That has such people in it![44]

How have these series of crises affected Australian society? How has society changed? If only the fittest survive in this brave new world, how will Australians continue to exploit the proven advantages they possess to assure their continuing survival? Knowledge and energy will not be enough; Australia's resources and national identity must be protected from those who would usurp them. The last four decades have been harrowing, but there will be even more bitter truths for Australia's people to accept in the years ahead.

Security threats

Only once in its history has the security of the Australian continent been under such threat as it is now; that was the attempted Japanese invasion during the Second World War. At that time, the intervention of the US navy saved the nation from invasion. Now, in 2053, with the USA enfeebled and fragmented, Australia has had to stand alone in responding to the global crisis.

This menace was not foreseen in defence planning. Prior to the crash of 2016 China was seen as a threat, not for any reason other

---

[44] William Shakespeare, *The Tempest*

than the strength of the military capability it had built, like its economy, in so short a time. Indonesia was also feared. There was an apprehension of being colonised, drawn into another 'South East Asian co-prosperity' sphere. But as climate change took its course, the perceived threat offered by other nation states in the region receded; with their inadequate finances, shattered industrial infrastructure and fragmented civil governments, they lost the capability to wage war.

Instead, Australian interests have been attacked by the many freelance militia outfits, mafias, pirate gangs and rogue warlord states which now thrive in the areas of the world where anarchy reigns. Cracks which have emerged in failed states, particularly in South America, Italy, Mexico, the Caucasus, China, most of Africa, and what was left of Russia, have allowed corrupt ruling elites, often mere criminal and pirate gangs, to emerge, and to rule ministates of their own. China is now fractured into a dozen regions, run by warlords leading remnants of the Red Army. Indonesia and the Philippines have disintegrated into hundreds of island statelets, with governments ranging from rudimentary democracies down to little more than mafia and triad gangs. The armouries of the world have been broken open and the world is awash with arms. Although the industrial capacity to build nuclear weapons has, for the moment, been lost in the chaos, a small number of devices have fallen into the wrong hands.

These anarchic elements present Australia with three major threats: illegal immigration, extortion by hostage-taking and the interruption of trade.

Multiple swarms of illegal immigrants island-hop through the northern archipelagos and then attempt to either cross the Timor Sea in small boats, or get to the southern coast in converted tramp freighters. Desperate, exploited people, they are led by ruthless pirates who probe and look for weaknesses in the border defences. These boats are relentlessly tracked by the navy, intercepted and either turned around or sunk. It is an enormous tragedy, but it is impossible for this already over-settled island to support any more people; it is either that, or ruin and death for the entire Australian population. These are the inescapable ethics of the 'lifeboat'.

Extortion has been a grim phenomenon in the tumultuous decades of the twenty-first century. It began in a small way with pirates taking individual ships hostage in exchange for payments of gold. It reached its climax with the tragedy of Darwin in 2040. Agents from Szechuan smuggled a suitcase-sized nuclear bomb into the city in a foreign cargo ship and hid it. They lodged a list of demands, including large quantities of gold, ships loaded with raw materials and long-range bomber aircraft. Just as negotiations were opening, the device detonated – by accident, it was thought – and the city was obliterated. Never again have foreign-flagged ships been allowed to enter the maritime exclusion area surrounding the coast. Never again have Australian-flagged ships been allowed to sail unescorted. All sea-borne freight, all exports and much of the imports, are now transported in convoys escorted by the navy. Foreign ships transporting to Australia must offload at Cocos or Norfolk Island for transhipment to Australia's own merchant fleet.

Response to the threats

Australia's empty northern frontiers and the desert interior once provided it with in-depth defence. Similarly, around the southern coast, the Bight presented a formidable obstacle of cliffs and desert. However, it was quickly realized that an obstacle does not remain an obstacle unless it is covered by observation and firepower. The lack of observation was soon overcome. Initially, light aircraft, abandoned in their hundreds after the Crash, were converted into robot drones equipped with cameras and surveillance equipment. It was necessary to patrol well off the coast, because ship-borne nuclear weapons have to be detected and destroyed well beyond detonation range of their intended coastal targets. Over time, drone aircraft that can be operated above the ceiling of the attackers' ground-to-air missiles have been designed and built.

After the Crash in 2016, international trade gradually resumed, initially on a basis of barter until the foreign currency trading system could be rebuilt. Australia's trade in 2053, limited compared to the levels of fifty years ago, is still essential both nationally and internationally. To assure security from pirates who now roam the high seas, defended convoys have been introduced. Early on, Australia saw that its shipbuilding capacity was inadequate to provide naval ships to protect the growing traffic, and again a home-designed adaptation of civil assets was resorted to. Disused ore carriers, of which there were many, were converted to helicopter carriers and missile platforms. They are slow, diesel-engine-driven monsters, but their missile payload capacity is prodigious compared to the sleek, fast warships, and their broad hulls provide a more stable surface for landing aircraft. In addition, they can be camouflaged for surprise offensive operations, at which they are particularly effective. Ironically, we may not have survived without the addition of the Pakistan Navy, which had been at sea on exercise when their country was destroyed by flood in 2020; when it became clear that their home port was lost, the fleet sailed to Fremantle and a new life.

For the first time in its history, the Australian Army is now deployed at home, defending the northern and eastern coasts against raids from marauding warlord gangs from the north. These mobs, like the Viking marauders of the Dark Ages, often deploy in battalion or division strength, travel in makeshift flotillas of small ships and attack either to plunder food and resources – equipment, cars and fuel – or to take hostages to exchange for more substantial needs. Unlike the terrorists of the late twentieth century, these are not ideologues, but desperate men striving to prevail in their own fiefdoms, campaigning with skill and cunning. Australia must surpass them in intelligence and ruthlessness if it wishes to protect what it has created.

Citizen military forces

But there is a need for vigilance in this reconstructed Australia. I believe there is a greater danger which has yet to be acknowledged: the risk that Australia's armed forces could become institutionalised and rise to dominate the state. The Roman Republic was organised on the principle of exerting maximum external threat, whilst assuring the rule of democracy uninfluenced by military power. This policy, successful at first, failed, just as the state reached its zenith at the hands of Julius Caesar. Switzerland, on the other hand, successfully balanced personal freedoms with armed inviolability for a millennia. It seems to me that the combination of a weak central government with a military organisation made up of citizens provides the checks and balances necessary to prevent military dictatorship; nevertheless, it is urgent that this issue, which was not foreseen in the 2020 constitutional convention, is formally addressed in Australia.

After the hedonistic apathy of the pre-Crash decades, Australia has, so far, experienced a resurgence of political awareness and dialogue. This reawakening of political consciousness has been driven by the complexities of the new system of county government and the setting up of many co-operative businesses. It is of utmost importance that Australia ensures that elites can never again grow to dominate the country. All citizens must be empowered and indeed motivated to participate in a hands-on democratic process. Training in the political arts – public speaking, personal development and effectiveness, coaching, leadership – once provided only by businesses to their employees, must continue to be available to all and included in basic schooling.

A reborn society

So what has been created by the people of this remote southern land? What kind of a society has emerged from the travails of economic hardship and climate change? What has been salvaged from the old world, and what has been preserved? What is there still to build?

Human society has seen a gradual reversal of the break-up of families and the atomisation of communities into individual units. Families were thrust together by crisis to support each other through loss, sickness, unemployment and poverty. Since the Crash of 2016, government social spending has all but disappeared; it had been supported for too long at unrealistic levels by excessive borrowing. Compensating for this, Australian society has experienced an upsurge in the number of community-funded welfare organisations, particularly for the care of the old and incapacitated, many of whom were left in poverty when their pensions were destroyed by the collapse of the stock market.

The break-up and dispersal of centralised offices, factories and plants coincided with an upsurge in the number of women working and taking management and leadership roles at all levels. Women are better than men at managing the increased integration of work, life and play. Local crèches have sprung up everywhere, so more parents can go to work and yet remain close to their children.

Australia's values have changed. The pursuit of money and the profit motive have taken a back seat to other values. John Stuart

Mill, writing in 1848, looked forward to the emergence of such a stationary economy:

> There would be as much scope as ever for all kinds of mental culture, and moral and social progress; as much room for improving the Art of Living and much more likelihood of it being improved, when minds cease to be engrossed by the art of getting on. Even the industrial arts might be as earnestly and as successfully cultivated, with this sole difference, that instead of serving no purpose but the increase of wealth, industrial improvements would produce their legitimate effect, that of abridging labour.[45]

Australia has successfully contrived to live without growth of population and money. The environmental rules made this inevitable. In the first years after 2016, times were tough and many people had to adapt to austerity. The greatest challenge was getting things organised; the beginning was an incredible period of change and innovation. It takes a lot of talking and listening for people to develop new ways of doing things, rather than checking in one's brain on entering the workplace, then to be told what to do by the boss. Management by committee was once considered undesirable and inefficient, but, with perseverance, it gives shared commitment and responsibility. When it is said that growth has ended in Australia, this does not mean that change has ended. Improvements in efficiency and innovations in technology and organisation allow more and more to be derived from the resources consumed. There are no limits to the growth of knowledge.

The Australian 'story' has been renewed. Now it incorporates the achievements of aboriginal society, the many migrant cultures acquired after European settlement, and an awareness of the

---

[45] John Stuart Mill, *Principles of Political Economy with some of their Applications to Social Philosophy*, Book IV, ChVI

uniqueness of its history and culture, with an enthusiasm that harks back to the nationalism of the late nineteenth century. It is now recognised that Australia has been richly endowed by nature and by the hard work and sacrifice of earlier Australians, heroes to whom veneration is owed. The Republic, forged in the Constitutional Convention of 2020, brings the best people and the best thinking to bear on the risks and opportunities Australia faces. The growing self-confidence and political activism of its citizens leaves no place for incompetent or self-seeking members of society to hide in self-absorbed, political game-playing. The issues are too great and urgent.

Economics is now a subsidiary discipline of science. Scientists set the rules on resource consumption and replacement, then economists and engineers determine how to conform to those limits, and how to innovate to achieve as much as possible from every gram of natural resources used. Now, government members are predominately experienced technocrats.

Australian life is no longer filled up with trivial pursuits. The kind of people who are revered are no longer the shallow types put forward by entertainment marketing men, but people of real accomplishment. Abolition of advertising had a lot to do with this. Even film and media stars are men and women of character and substance. The arts thrive as never before; with more free time, there has developed a thirst for life-enhancing film, music and art.

With more free time, sporting activities, always a passion, have become even more important in the lives and health of Australians. The people are less and less guilty of being mere onlookers; spectator activity has reduced as participation has increased, fuelled by greater investment in community facilities. With limits to income, the sports of the rich, such as golf and skiing, are no longer affordable, nor are the environmental impacts of their excessive land use acceptable. The exception to this remains horse racing; the rearing and riding of horses taps a deep root in human history.

Husbandry of knowledge

Education and the acquisition of knowledge has become ever more important as the quantity of what a person owns has been superseded by the merit of who a person is. Education in Australia is controlled at county level, as with business and commerce, resulting in an improved alignment between what is taught and the skills wanted by society. Full-time education still spans the ages of five to eighteen, but there has been a huge increase in continuing education for adults; each Australian adult citizen is now entitled to attend one month of further education per year, in addition to one month of paid vacation.

After the Crash of 2016, when it became clear that the world was approaching a crisis point, Australia's universities launched a successful collaboration project to gather all the world's knowledge, literature and arts into a virtual library accessible by the national information network. Multiple copies of the database exist in digital form in various media across the country, and a physical microfilm version is stored in vaults deep below the Snowy Mountains.

Australia is not just preserving knowledge, or mining the knowledge which has been so carefully stored in many repositories; knowledge through original research is also being created. Investigations devoted to gaining understanding for its own sake – the 'pure' disciplines – are as numerous as those devoted to 'applied' research; the latter is very much focused on improvements in efficiency that will enhance the well-being of society or reduce its impact on the planet. Knowledge is no longer power; it is shared with other specialists working elsewhere in the world, by correspondence and often by travel.

Medical research continues to support medical professions freed from the profit motive and dedicated solely to excellence. In this case, excellence is, as always, the promotion of well-being, but with an aging population, the understanding and treatment of degenerative diseases assumes greater importance.

Biology, energy and the earth sciences have flourished. Biological research in Australia has achieved some remarkable results in agriculture, and at cell level, expanding the existing knowledge and understanding of the biomes of plants and animals, and acquiring remarkable new insights into quantum biology. Discoveries in genetics and quantum biology, when applied to medicine, have shone a light on the understanding of the human biome and body. Great progress is still being made in understanding the bacterial origins and treatments of diseases. In an interesting fusion of art and science, the discipline of genetic archaeology has developed to a point where we can now track the sequence of evolution of a species from its ancient ancestors.

Law and order

One of the enduring strengths of Australian society is the rule of law, especially through a time of great stress that obliterated law and order in many parts of the world. Australia's legal system has always been adversarial, not only supporting but often encouraging conflict, unlike others such as the Napoleonic or Sharia systems. With austerity, and the limits imposed on personal income, the Australian approach to the law has become more conciliatory. Australia did, after all, establish a unique approach to the conciliation and arbitration of industrial arguments, which, in recent years, has been extended to many other aspects of the law and human relationships. Concern for the social benefits of dispute resolution has replaced the winner-takes-all contest of the court room.

Crime and criminal law is something Australian society continues to have to live with, although the frequency of crime has diminished. An aging but still active population, slowly growing in collective wisdom, can explain the reduction in crimes of violence. There has been a decrease in sex crimes, attributed to an increase in sexual freedom, stemming from much more aggressive birth control and the sense that, during several horrifying periods, the end of the world was at hand. Although people have worked together in the face of common threats, an upsurge in fraud and commercial crime has resulted from the limits placed on personal income. Taxation of consumption has led to the black economy being replaced by a black market; thus, tax evasion and crime are still unacceptably high.

The nation's revised infrastructure

The shape of cities and towns has changed. The idea of localism, developed in response to the need for greater personal productivity has brought businesses back to the people; this, in turn, has discouraged excessive mobility and restored the very satisfying feeling of living in a big village. Local shopping, pubs and cafes have returned to the high streets and corners. The redirection of capital investment away from business to permanent community assets has led to an increase in local function rooms, sporting facilities and arts venues, important places in a society in which work is rationed, home life is more austere and people have more time to devote to recreation and their pastimes. As much as possible, existing buildings are preserved and maintained. New house construction, after a brief boom because of migration back to the country areas, has declined, and is now restricted to the replacement of dwellings beyond repair.

The existing road system in Australia is perfectly adequate for its citizens' needs, with a limited amount of construction work devoted to safety black spots and points of congestion. Most recent infrastructure construction investment has been on electric power systems, information systems and the rail network. The high speed train system, begun when ash from the South American volcanoes, erupting in 2031, grounded jet aircraft travel for a decade, now links all the nation's state capitals.

Personal taxation is now predominantly on spending. In the years since the income tax threshold was increased to 100% at ten times the minimum wage, proceeds have dwindled to zero. The maximum sum that any citizen can earn has now been effectively capped at ten times the minimum. When introduced in 2021, many argued that limiting income would remove incentives for excellence; quite the opposite has happened as less selfish and more public-minded leaders have stepped forward to fill the shoes of the oligarchs and kleptocrats. Taxes are collected at county level, and allocations made annually to states, and from states to the national government.

Resources are taxed at the point at which they are extracted from the biosphere, as are all discharges back to the biosphere. This encourages people to add as much value as they can to the resources they work with, and to reduce what they dump to the lowest possible level.

A great increase in microfinance as a proportion of national lending has been the result of restricting the registration and activities of banks to individual counties. Both lending and borrowing in Australia are now conducted more responsibly in a village-like environment where everyone knows what everyone else is up to.

Disorganised religion

One of my predominant themes has been the question: how could sapient people, foreseeing the future as they did, have allowed this to happen? For some, an even bigger question is, how could God have let this happen? Organised religions were among the leading institutions of the last millennia, standing on a level with national governments, multinational corporations, and the global media. Yet they stood back helplessly with their feet in the Bronze Age and their heads in the Middle Ages, wringing their hands while the world collapsed.

The events of the last fifty years have polarised mankind's attitude to God. At one pole are those who seek answers to the great mysteries of nature in the study of science and knowledge, and at the other are those whose religious faith, forged by catastrophe, has become stronger. My own life has been a quest for understanding, and the more I learned, the more I realised that I cannot even conceive of what it is I don't know.

> There are more things in heaven and earth, Horatio, than are dreamed of in thy philosophy.[46]

Looking back at the steps in the evolution of the human brain, from the cell wall to reptilian, mammalian, neo-cortical, and with it the development of consciousness, or what the Jesuit anthropologist Pierre Teilhard de Chardin called the 'within', I cannot even imagine how life began or how it might evolve.

The effete old men of the Vatican and the adamant priests of Wahab assert that God created man. I look around at the myriad forms of religion in this world and see only gods created by man. It is absurd to me to read so many differing versions of the absolute truth. Each religion, in my opinion, presents a

---

[46] William Shakespeare, *Hamlet*

speculative view of why things are the way they are, framed in an earlier era, committed to books and doomed to become dogma – in contrast to the scientific method, where speculation is only the first stage, followed by the second, which attempts to gain certainty through experimental proof.

In my view, religion failed and continues to fail the world in this crisis. The whole point of morality, other than assuring us that our souls shall go to heaven, is arguably to ensure the survival of the race. By encouraging population growth, religion continued to promote an outmoded morality designed to assure the survival of man in a hostile world; hence, the strictures of the Vatican on contraception, birth control, and single-sex relationships were completely inappropriate for an overpopulated world. If our morality says that we must not restrict population growth to assure the survival of the race and all the other species of life on the planet, then I believe that morality is wrong and should be changed.

The Christian church failed as a guide to morality through an inability to reconcile its theology with the truths of science. Instead, it continued to promulgate its understanding of the biblical age and the disputes of the eternally quarrelsome people of Palestine. In Australia, the once-powerful churches are now weakened and their teachings largely ignored. The foundations and institutions – schools, hospitals, hospices, and the like – which they sponsored, continue to evince respect for the good works performed by so many dedicated and unselfish people.

Similarly, science failed to reconcile its philosophy of demonstrable truth with the spiritual mysteries. Science seeks to understand the 'unknown', but unless it can reconcile itself with uncertainty, accepting that the 'unknown' may be inconceivably different from what is now known, it may not progress to greater levels of understanding; consider, for example, the intense discomfort of science with quantum biology.

Although some people regret the loss of certainty which the church provided through the ages, I believe that the deep introspection and questioning which preoccupy so many religions now is a healthy trend; there is still a limitless need for goodness and excellence in human lives, and for a new theology of confident speculation, in place of the defensive bigotry that once passed for our thinking about God.

A charter for the future

In the last decades, a new morality has emerged, in the spirit of the Earth Charter. Australia was first to adopt, in 2020, the Earth Charter[47] as part of the declaration of rights forming the preamble to the second federal constitution. It acknowledges the right of mankind to life, but not at the expense of the race or of other species – the right to exist without unbalancing the cycles of nature.

We must understand that the processes of nature will change the Earth beyond our understanding or control, and that we must be prepared to adapt ourselves for survival in an Earth that may be hotter, colder, drier or wetter, just as we have had to adjust to the change from the interglacial to the new glaciation. Only when our level of consciousness and understanding embraces the complexity of the Earth's systems should we attempt to harness the forces of nature.

---

[47] www.earthcharterinaction.org

The most fortunate of people.

The world could have taken many different directions than that of global cooling. Glaciation could have been more severe, with all human activity frozen to a standstill. At the other extreme, if volcanic activity had been delayed, we could have experienced the sudden catastrophic release of marine clathrates and tundra gases, causing such rapid heating that the climate of the world could have reverted to a state similar to the Paleocene-Eocene thermal maximum, with polar ice caps melted, mankind extinct with many other species, and evolution set back by 56 million years.

Humanity, for all the wonders of its civilisations, science, arts and systems of justice, is just as susceptible to uncontrolled growth and collapse as a bell jar full of fruit flies and syrup. Even the most sophisticated of human organisations is incapable of the kind of restraint and forethought required for sustained existence. Our species could very well have returned to a tribal, brutal form of existence, the one for which our genes have equipped us. A small group of survivors could have clung on and lived in an archaic manner.

Mankind has been in this situation before, in the centuries after the Toba eruption. To survive, it must rise beyond the genetic equipment that nearly led to downfall and adopt a more altruistic basis for life, in which the ethos of human behaviour is the greatest benefit for as many souls as the world can *sustainably* support into the infinite future.

POSTSCRIPT

Australia Felix

The title of this work is of course a play on the appellation given by the Scots explorer Thomas Mitchell when he first set eyes on the sunlit plains of central Victoria.

> The region he had now entered was to be named later, in the spring, as he departed from it; and its name, chosen to describe so fertile and favourable a tract, a land blessed by fortune, was Australia Felix.[48]

At this time the vast green plains were still husbanded by the aboriginal people. They reminded Mitchell of the grand estates of Britiain. The term Australia Felix, the blessed, in later parlance became the Lucky Country.

The phoenix is a long-lived bird associated with the sun, originating from ancient Egyptian mythology. According to the ancient belief, it is cyclically regenerated or reborn, arising from the ashes of its predecessor.

The miracle of survival and rebirth has been repeated in a score or more of places around the world. Each has their own story to tell. And although each approached the catastrophe with a robust society and collective genius, those who survived did so only through luck, being in the right place geographically at the right time. It wasn't through skill ... only luck.

Is it acceptable that a species and a civilisation depends on chance for their existence?

---

[48] *Stapylton – With Major Mitchell's Australia Felix Expedition 1836*, edited by Alan E. J. Andrews

ABOUT THE AUTHOR

David Morgan was born in Mooroopna in 1951 and grew up in rural Victoria. He graduated with a degree in Civil Engineering from Melbourne and was commissioned in the army reserve in 1973. He worked for a number of multi-national corporations during a career in engineering and construction which spanned the world. Latterly he led major development projects in the upstream oil and gas industry. He retired early because of Parkinson's Disease and now lives with his wife in the south-west of France, where he paints, writes and gardens.

Made in the USA
Charleston, SC
26 May 2013